THE
SUNSHINE
DIET

SHELINA PERMALLOO

THE
SUNSHINE
DIET

Get some sunshine into your life,
lose weight and feel amazing

SHELINA PERMALLOO

EBURY
PRESS

10 9 8 7 6 5 4 3 2 1

Ebury Press, an imprint of Ebury Publishing
20 Vauxhall Bridge Road, London, SW1V 2SA

Ebury Press is part of the Penguin Random House group of companies
whose addresses can be found at global.penguinrandomhouse.com

Penguin
Random House
UK

First published by Ebury Press in 2015

www.eburypublishing.co.uk

A CIP catalogue record for this book is available from the British
Library

ISBN: 9780091951146

Design: Smith and Gilmour
Photography: Martin Poole
Food stylist: Aya Nishimura
Stylist: Jo Harris, Lydia Brun and Jessica Georgiades

Colour reproduction: Altaimage
Printed and bound in China by C&C Offset Printing Co., Ltd.

Penguin Random House is committed to a sustainable future for
our business, our readers and our planet. This book is made from
Forest Stewardship Council® certified paper.

contents

INTRODUCTION

Winning *MasterChef* in 2012 was one of the best experiences of my life. I remember John and Gregg describing my food as 'sunshine on a plate' and that I was 'a restaurant waiting to happen'. I called my first cookbook *Sunshine on a Plate* and I'm working on that restaurant dream!

In the final of the show, they asked me what I wanted my food to 'do'. I remember saying that I would like them to eat my food and feel transported to their favourite holiday destination, to feel the sun beating down on them and sand between their toes, with the best holiday food in front of them. This is the sort of food I've always loved to cook and share with family and friends.

After *MasterChef*, I was thrown full throttle into the food industry, cooking live on television and touring the country for book signings, private cooking events and food festivals, plus I was flying back to Mauritius every so often for work events. It was a hectic couple of years but I absolutely loved every minute.

When there are so many positives in your life, there is always likely to be a negative, and for me it was weight gain. If you're anything like me and love food as much as I do, it can be quite easy to get distracted by all the other things going on in life and stop paying attention to what and how much you're eating. I knew I needed to get a healthy balance back in my life, but I also wanted to find a way of having my cake and eating it!

Getting back to feeling like 'me'

I remember being involved in a photo shoot in early 2013, and looking in the mirror and feeling that I didn't look like 'me' anymore. Shopping for clothes at the time wasn't much fun either as it was difficult to find something I liked that also fitted. I knew then that I had to do something to get back to looking healthy and feeling good about myself, so I made some changes:

* I started walking as much as possible, instead of driving or using public transport; this really helped and I enjoyed the time it gave me to think, too.
* I started paying more attention to the way I ate.
* I made sure that I spent more time planning what I was going to eat, so as to avoid snacking on food throughout the day or, worse still, not eating much during the day and then overindulging in the evening.
* I chose food that was packed with goodness as well as tasting delicious.
* I chose low-fat options, bulking up my meals with salads, vegetables and lean protein.
* I enjoyed fruit-based and low-sugar puddings when I fancied something sweet to eat.
* I found that eating four to five small meals throughout the day worked best for me.

Throughout this book, you'll find all the recipes I created and used to help me get back into shape and look and feel better too. In the process of writing this book, I've lost an amazing 20.5kg (45lb), so I now feel great, my skin glows, my hair feels strong and I just have so much energy.

Healthy food not diet food

Thanks to my Mauritian heritage, the food I love most is a fusion of flavours and a wonderful assault on the senses, influenced by French, African, Indian and Chinese cultures. My recipes celebrate the freshest of ingredients, including chillies and peppers, aromatic herbs and spices, vegetables, meat, fish and seafood and, of course, wonderfully tropical fruit, all accompanied by punchy condiments to create dishes offering that mouth-watering combination of tastes in every bite. Use more of these natural ingredients, plus herbs and spices, and you'll notice that you'll use less flavour enhancers like salt and other processed seasonings.

I am lucky enough to have friends who come from all walks of life, and this has really influenced the type of food I like to cook at home and what you'll find in this book. I fell in love with the fresh flavours of the food in Thailand, for example, when I visited, and realised how easy it is to cook and enjoy healthy food there. You get that sensation of hot, sour, salty and sweet that leaves you feeling full and satisfied. You'll find that balance of flavours a lot in my recipes; even the sweet ones were created with the same thought process.

Even though this book is called *The Sunshine Diet*, it's important for me to reiterate that this isn't a diet book in the typical sense. This is my alternative to the restrictive diet books that dictate what you eat! I would like this book to inspire you to cook healthy food that doesn't compromise at all on flavour, so that you can keep enjoying food, while looking and feeling your best too.

A conventional diet book will give you a structured and almost dictatorial way of eating. But I take a very different approach and feel that good health is about having fun, eating well and living well and, perhaps most importantly of all, it's about the enjoyment of preparing, cooking and serving delicious and healthy food for yourself, your family and your friends, that won't leave you feeling guilty. By including these recipes as part of your everyday eating, I am confident that you'll see the weight gradually drop off. Perhaps the best part is that your confidence will grow and you will hear people say things like 'you look glowing' and 'you seem so happy', and that's what great food does to you.

My healthy eating plan is simple

* Eat everything in moderation, choose ingredients that are delicious but won't impact negatively on your health.

* Pack flavour into dishes using fresh ingredients like fresh herbs and spices, citrus fruit juices and chillies, and use the natural sugars found in fruit to add sweetness (see page 13 for more information on healthy ingredients).
* Colour is as important as taste – you eat with your eyes, too – so cook with a range of ingredients that make the plate look vibrant and appealing.
* I like to mix and match what I eat during the week; sometimes I have a meat-free day or avoid carbohydrates and fill up on lean protein and vegetables instead. Keeping your diet varied, keeps it interesting.
* Whatever you fancy, aim to fill up on natural, nutritious whole foods. Prepare as much as you can from scratch, including making dishes in advance if you know you have a busy week ahead.
* It's important that you treat yourself every so often, so don't hold back on desserts.
* I want you to mix and match the recipes in this book as much as you fancy, so I haven't included any strict diet plans. However, here are a few examples of how I like to mix up some of the recipes in this book so that I ensure I get a variety of nutrients every day in a way that works for me.

A typical weekday

I think it's important that I treat every day as different, as my work schedule can vary so much it's hard to know whether it's a weekday or the weekend. Whatever day it is, don't deprive yourself on flavour. If you eat a treat pudding then try to pack in as much fruit and vegetables as possible, and perhaps opt for a lower carb day. A typical weekday menu for me might include:

Breakfast: *Beet and Ginger Smoothie* (page 36)
Lunch: *Chicken and Green Mango Salad* (page 48)
Dinner: *Hake with Wasabi, Soy and Ginger* (page 63)
Dessert: *Lemon Verbena & Rose Petal Jellies* (page 180)

A meat-free day

I love fruit and vegetables and tend to have quite a few meat-free days in my typical week. The salad section of this book is full of interesting flavours for lunch while something like okra and beans make a hearty dinner that won't leave you feeling like you're missing out. Try the following meat-free menu:

Breakfast: *Breakfast Cous Cous with Dried Fruit* (page 25)
Lunch: *Caribbean Allspice Salad with Pumpkin and Black Beans* (page 76)
Dinner: *Chana Dahl and Curry Leaves* (page 96)

At the weekend

I like to start my day in a more leisurely fashion at the weekends, swapping breakfast for brunch and treating myself in the evening to a tasty pud. An ideal weekend menu for me might include:

Brunch: *Baked Moroccan Eggs* (page 43)
Light late lunch: *Flaked Mackerel with Lemon and Fennel* (page 64)
Dinner: *Beef with Lemon Grass and Sichuan Pepper (page 165)*
Dessert: *Halo Halo* (page 208)

I think there is no substitute for water in keeping you hydraded. Keep topping up a small bottle of water and keep it near you. Sometimes we feel hungry when in fact we are just thirsty. Knowing the difference will definitely affect your diet.

Managing weight loss

To help you get that balance right, I've included calorie, fat and sugar counts with every recipe in this book, but personally I don't think calorie counting is the best way to manage weight loss. It's all too easy to fixate on calories and lose sight of what you're actually eating and whether it's really good for your body. Even if you are trying to lose weight, you need to eat nourishing real foods to give you energy throughout the day and keep you healthy from the inside-out. There's no big secret to how dieting works; in the simplest form it is means cutting down on various things, especially fatty and high carbohydrate foods. Fruits and vegetables are really good for us, and increasing your intake of these will make you feel great.

I really hope you enjoy cooking these fabulous recipes as much as I do, and I am confident that you will! Food is my life; after all, what is the point of eating food if it doesn't excite and satisfy you?

My favourite healthy ingredients

Simple natural flavourings will add wonderful depth and layers of flavour to your food, as well as a variety of nutrients. I've listed other common ingredients you'll find in this book and explained why I love to cook with them.

Spices

Chillies contain high levels of vitamins and minerals and fresh chillies, in particular, are a good source of vitamin C. I like to use bird's eye chilli, which are small, thin, red or green chillies and very hot. If you can't find bird's eye chillies you can use the larger chillies instead. (See also Recipe Notes, page 17, on deseeding chillies.) I use sweet, smoky and fragrant **cinnamon** in both savoury and sweet dishes. Cinnamon has been linked to lowering cholesterol, and some studies have shown that it can lower blood sugar levels by increasing insulin production in the body. **Coriander seeds** are warm and nutty. You can buy ground coriander or grind the seeds yourself in a spice grinder or using a pestle and mortar. Use toasted **cumin** and **mustard**

seeds to season dishes and add subtle flavouring to rice and curries (see Recipe Notes on how to toast seeds). Fresh root **ginger** is probably the spice that I use most often for its health benefits. Not only does it help to combat the common cold, it also aids digestion and can prevent nausea, but the reason I use it so often is because it is high in antioxidants and cleanses the system of toxins. **Turmeric**, a bright yellow powder, creates colour and imparts an earthy and sharp flavour. Turmeric is thought to be high in antioxidants and therefore is used across the globe as a great way of defending the body and boosting the immune system. When I was growing up my Mum used to boil milk and add ginger, black peppercorns and turmeric, and this was to ward off the common cold, but I also find turmeric helps to make my skin gleam. I still drink milk and turmeric occasionally to give me that wonderful glow!

Herbs

Use **fresh coriander** leaves and stalks to flavour and garnish dishes. I tend to buy it in bunches and store it in the fridge, wrapped in a damp cloth. **Parsley** features in quite a few dishes – more typically in those influenced by Mediterranean cuisines. As with fresh coriander, you can buy it in bunches and keep it for several days in a glass of water or in the fridge, wrapped in a damp cloth. **Thyme** is a classic European herb that's used a lot in French and Portuguese cooking. It's often found in stews and curries, and I like to add it to braised meat. **Mint** is the herb I love to throw in so many dishes – I love its menthol quality and how it can be both subtle and daring in a dish; add as little or as much as you like. Mint is a good digestion aid.

Flavourings

Coconut water is deliciously refreshing and has a unique sweet and sour taste. It's naturally hydrating because it is rich in electrolytes. Liquidised fresh **coconut flesh** is brilliant as a dairy substitute for people who are lactose intolerant or avoiding dairy. A lot of my recipes use fresh **garlic**, and sometimes lots of it. Garlic is a good base flavour but also has a number of associated health benefits, including the strengthening of the blood system and helping to lower cholesterol. For the brave, the health benefits of garlic are increased when it is eaten raw, so my Harissa paste and Nam Pla Prik recipes on pages 212 and 217 are perfect!

I use good-quality **vanilla** extract or vanilla pods from such producers as Nielsen-Massey or vanilla from Madagascar. Always keep the vanilla pod once you have removed the seeds – you can add it to a jar of caster sugar to make vanilla sugar, or even to a bottle of rum! (See Recipe Notes on page 17 for how to remove the seeds.)

Oils, meat, fish and dairy

We need some fat in our diet to stay healthy, and a little oil goes a long way, so don't avoid it completely. I use **olive oil**, **vegetable oil** and sometimes **coconut**, **mustard** or **sesame oil** for cooking. I also use **rapeseed** and **extra virgin olive oil** for dressings. When it comes to meat, I choose lean cuts such as **chicken, beef sirloin**, **pork tenderloin, rabbit** and **turkey**. **Braising steak** and **leg of lamb** are both good slow-cook crowd pleasers that can stretch to feed a lot of people. I eat many different kinds of fish, enjoying the omega-3 fatty acids in **herring**, **mackerel**, **salmon** and **sardines**, as well as the lean protein of white fish such as **cod**, **hake**, **sea bass** and **sea bream** and iron-rich **tuna**. Low-fat seafood and shellfish, including **lobster**, **mussels**, **prawns** and **squid**, are all great. In general, I use reduced-fat, 0% fat and low-fat **dairy** products but occasionally I enjoy one of the treat puddings in this book that contain cream! I crumble **full-fat feta** or include **haloumi** in dishes – you don't need much to add heaps of flavour. I also use reduced-fat **coconut milk** as an alternative to dairy.

Pulses and beans

Pulses and beans are all great sources of protein and energy-giving carbohydrates. I use **yellow split peas, yellow and brown lentils, bulgar wheat, broad beans, black-eyed beans, black beans, red kidney beans and chickpeas** to bulk up dishes so I feel fuller for longer.

Shopping Tips

The most important thing to get across is that I would like you to get excited about food again and really enjoy what you eat! Go out to markets and see what you can find; pick up fruit and vegetables and smell them, feel them. Experiment with fresh new flavours and textures. Buy the best quality and freshest ingredients you can afford.

I always find that when I go to the market I save so much money too. My best tip when buying protein is always to buy a bigger piece and then divide it up into portions: buy a whole chicken, then joint it yourself at home. It's much more economical this way. I use the wings and bones for stock, the breasts for salads and grilling, then the darker meat for stews, curries and braises.

Also, there is no harm in using frozen vegetables or fruit such as mixed berries, which are perfect for freezing, and sweetcorn, peas and hardier herbs such as thyme and rosemary all freeze well too.

Buying Spices

Don't go for big spice packs just because they are more economical. It's important that your spices are fresh and don't dry out; as they dry they lose their oils and flavour, so older spices become less fragrant and aromatic. Buy smaller quantities as and when you need them, and store them in airtight containers in a cool, dry, dark place. For best flavour, buy whole spices and grind them yourself.

Recipe Notes

* All eggs are medium and organic or free-range.
* I use Billington's unrefined sugars. I always use unrefined sugar when I'm cooking, baking and making sweet treats. Unrefined sugar is natural and has not been processed, which also means that a little goes a long way. If you can, always opt for this and you'll notice the difference in flavour straight away.
* I use Koko coconut milk whenever I need light coconut milk because it is lower in fat and calories than other light coconut milks but still tastes creamy and rich.
* I use fresh chillies in many of my recipes, and I usually like to leave the seeds in (except in salads) because I like the heat. Depending on how much heat you like, you can always deseed them before using, if you prefer. In the majority of my recipes, I don't specify.
* *To prepare dried red chillies*: put the dried chillies into a bowl, cover with hot water and leave to soak for 15 minutes. Drain well and pat dry, then use as required.
* *To remove seeds from a vanilla pod*: place the pod on a chopping board, and using the flat side of a knife blade, press firmly along the whole pod to flatten it. Cut or split the pod in half lengthways and then scrape out the seeds using the sharp edge or tip of the knife.
* *To toast seeds*: heat a small, heavy-based frying pan over a high heat (do not add any oil), add the seeds and leave to toast for a minute or so until the seeds start to become fragrant and begin to release their oils, shaking the pan once or twice. Remove from the pan and leave to cool, then use whole or grind the seeds to a coarse powder using a pestle and mortar.
* In all my recipes, I use non-stick cookware and bakeware, so all pots, pans (saucepans, frying pans, griddle pans, woks), baking trays and roasting tins are non-stick as this helps to reduce the amount of oil needed.

BREAKFAST
& BRUNCH

'Whatever you fancy, aim to fill up on natural, nutritious whole foods.'

BREAKFAST & BRUNCH

Breakfast is such an important part of the day. To be honest, the time my weight used to yoyo around was on the weeks I didn't manage to squeeze in a good breakfast. It doesn't have to be extravagant or time consuming, but it does have to be nourishing. Depending on the weather I tend to select my breakfasts differently: cold weather always calls for something warmer and more filling; on sunnier, warmer days I like a smoothie, a coconut milk or my Spanish toast.

One those days I really don't have time for breakfast, I have brunch instead. Brunch time for me is about 11 o'clock; cereal won't cut it, but I'm not hungry enough for lunch! I also like to have brunch when friends and family pop over in the mornings, usually before a leisurely walk through the park with a load of kids in tow.

You'll find a range of savoury and sweet ideas for breakfast and brunch here. All these recipes are easy to prepare and packed full of fresh flavours and a range of different food types to help boost energy levels. Foods that contain protein, such as eggs, low-fat dairy and beans are all great ways to start the day as they help to keep you fuller for longer. I've also included plenty of fruit and vegetables to maximise vitamins, minerals and fibre and I suggest that you serve granary and wholemeal breads on the side, which will provide energy as well as being packed with B vitamins. The great thing is no one will even notice that you've made a lighter option, and you'll feel set up for the day.

Yoghurt Pancakes with Blueberries

These are amazing, I mean seriously amazing, so if you've never made pancakes with yoghurt before you have to try these. They are thick and delicious and taste like pancakes but have the thickness of, say, a crumpet. These pancakes are also simple to make and are very moreish and satisfying, so do try them for yourself.

MAKES 8 PANCAKES

PER SERVING:
CALORIES 131KCAL
FAT 1G
SUGAR 6G

FOR THE PANCAKES
200g plain wholemeal flour
1½ tsp baking powder
¼ tsp bicarbonate of soda
125g fat-free Greek-style
    yoghurt
75g blueberries
115ml skimmed milk
1 egg
2 tbsp agave nectar
½ tsp vanilla extract
pinch of salt

TO SERVE (OPTIONAL)
Papaya and Pineapple Compote
    (see page 24) or fresh fruit
    and honey.

• •

Mix all the pancake ingredients together in a mixing bowl until well combined (the batter will be thick). Leave to stand for 10 minutes.

Heat a skillet or pancake pan over a medium to high heat until nearly smoking. For each pancake, spoon around 3 generous tablespoons of the mixture into the hot pan, gently spreading it out to about 8cm in diameter (each pancake will be thick). Leave it to cook for 3–4 minutes on one side. Once you start seeing bubbles appear on the surface and the underside is golden, it's ready to flip. Carefully turn the pancake over and cook the other side for another 3–4 minutes until golden brown.

Transfer the cooked pancake to a plate, cover with foil and keep warm, while you cook the remaining pancakes in the same way (to make 8 in total).

Serve the pancakes on their own or, if you like, serve with some papaya and pineapple compote spooned over or with fresh fruit and a drizzle of honey.

Papaya and Pineapple Compote

Serve this fruity, spicy compote with fat-free yoghurt or my Yoghurt Pancakes with Blueberries (see page 22).

(see page 22).

MAKES 700 GRAMS

PER SERVING:
CALORIES 66KCAL
FAT 0.3G
SUGAR 13G

2 small ripe papayas, peeled, seeded and cut into 2.5cm cubes
½ fresh small pineapple, peeled, cored and cut into 2.5cm cubes
75g unrefined molasses sugar
2 star anise
1 cinnamon stick
1 tsp ground mixed spice
50ml orange juice

Put all the ingredients into a medium pan and cook over a medium-low heat, stirring occasionally, for around 30 minutes until the compote is warmed through, being careful not to let the mixture catch on the bottom of the pan.

Remove from the heat and leave the compote to cool completely, then pour it into a sterilised jar, cover and store in the fridge. This compote will keep for up to a week in the fridge.

Breakfast Berry Rice

To my mind this is a winter breakfast, ideal for those days when it's grey and miserable outside: it is warm, filling, sweet and delicious. There's no better way to start the day when the weather is so grim.

SERVES 3

PER SERVING:
CALORIES 252KCAL
FAT 1G
SUGAR 27G

100g brown long-grain rice
450ml skimmed milk
3 tbsp unrefined light muscovado sugar
1 tsp good-quality vanilla extract (such as Neilsen-Massey)

TO SERVE
mixed fresh berries (such as raspberries, blueberries and strawberries)
6 tbsp light coconut milk

Put the rice, milk, sugar and vanilla extract into a heavy-based saucepan and cook over a medium heat for around 40 minutes, stirring occasionally, until the rice is cooked and tender and the mixture has thickened. Stir in a little water if the mixture begins to dry out.

Remove from the heat. Divide the rice mixture between 3 bowls and then top each portion with some mixed berries and 2 tablespoons of coconut milk. Serve immediately.

Breakfast Couscous SCENT OF THE SOUKS

This is such a different way to eat couscous, and I love the way you can easily transform wholemeal couscous into a sparkling breakfast full of eastern promise. I love orange blossom water because it reminds me of the wonderful scent of the souks I walked through in Marrakesh and all the stands that sold the dried fruit, nuts, honey and spices, with an overwhelming sweet smell of orange blossom all around.

This breakfast is filling and nutritious and will keep you full until lunchtime. It is also the perfect after-school snack for kids.

SERVES 4

PER SERVING:
CALORIES 170KCAL
FAT 0.3G
SUGAR 4G

200g wholemeal couscous
200ml boiling water
1 tbsp agave nectar
1 tbsp ground cinnamon
½ tsp orange blossom water

TO SERVE
mixed fresh berries and/
    or sliced stone fruit
    (such as raspberries,
    blueberries, nectarines,
    peaches, plums)
2 tbsp chopped pistachios
2 tbsp freshly shredded coconut

• • • ·· • •• ··· • •• · • •• ·· • •• ··· • •• ·· • •• ·· • •• ··· • •• ·

Put the couscous into a heatproof bowl and pour over the boiling water. Stir in the agave nectar, cinnamon and orange blossom water, then cover and leave to stand for about 5 minutes. Once all the water is absorbed, fluff up the couscous with a fork.

Divide the couscous between 4 bowls and then top with the fresh fruit, pistachios and coconut to serve.

Make-ahead Banana Bread

Banana bread is a staple in my house, and it is the ideal way to use up overripe bananas or ones that got a bit bruised on the way home from the shops. This is a no-fuss, easy to make ahead banana bread that is perfect for breakfast. I've added seeds and use wholemeal flour to make it nutritious and filling. I also love the way this makes the house smell deliciously sweet and spicy. You really do have to give this a go!

SERVES 8

PER SERVING:
CALORIES 297KCAL
FAT 9G
SUGAR 26G

50g unsalted butter, softened
125g unrefined golden caster sugar
1 egg
225g plain wholemeal flour
pinch of salt
1 tbsp ground mixed spice
2 tsp baking powder
1 tsp bicarbonate of soda
2–3 tbsp skimmed milk, to loosen the batter
4 bananas, peeled and crushed with the back of a fork
75g mixed seeds (I like to use a combination of pumpkin and nigella seeds)

• •

Preheat the oven to 180°C/gas 4. Lightly grease and line a 23 x 15cm loaf tin and set aside.

Using an electric stand mixer, whisk together the butter and sugar until light and fluffy. Crack in the egg and mix until combined. Add the flour, salt, mixed spice, baking powder and bicarbonate of soda and lightly fold in, adding enough milk to loosen the batter so that it drops off a spoon easily. Stir in the crushed bananas. Spoon the mixture evenly into the prepared loaf tin, then sprinkle the mixed seeds over the top.

Bake in the preheated oven for 40–50 minutes or until the banana bread is cooked and a skewer inserted into the centre comes out clean.

Remove from the oven and leave to cool slightly in the tin, then turn out onto a wire rack and leave to cool. Eat immediately while the bread is still warm, or leave to cool completely and keep in an airtight container.

Spanish Tomato Breakfast Toast

Whenever I go to Spain I love having this for breakfast because it's so simple. It makes the most of fresh, flavourful ingredients and doesn't need anything else. That's one thing I love about Spanish food, its pure simplicity.

Traditionally, the ingredients are just rubbed over the bread/toast, but here I like to prepare and mix the tomato topping beforehand and then spread it over the bread/toast. I always make more than I need as well, because the tomato mixture also makes a tasty dressing/sauce, ideal tossed with warm wholemeal pasta, if you fancy a quick bite to eat.

SERVES 2

PER SERVING:
CALORIES 140KCAL
FAT 7G
SUGAR 4G

3 plum tomatoes
1 small garlic clove, peeled
1 tbsp olive oil

pinch of salt
2 slices pumpernickel bread

•• ···· •• ···· • ···· • ···· • ···· •• ···· •• ···· •• ··· •

Finely chop the tomatoes and garlic and place in a bowl. Stir in the olive oil and salt, then leave to stand for around 15 minutes. Drain off some of the excess juice from the tomato mixture before you serve it.

Warm or toast the bread slices, top with the tomato mixture and eat straight away.

Roasted Aubergines with Fennel and Labneh

Labneh is a wonderful Middle Eastern strained yoghurt that is really easy to make and is a healthier alternative to soured cream or cream cheese. It usually takes around 12 hours to make, so it's best to prepare it the night before and leave it to drain in the fridge overnight. You will also need a piece of muslin.

SERVES 4

PER SERVING:
CALORIES 160KCAL
FAT 5G
SUGAR 10G

1 tsp salt
450g 0%-fat Greek-style
   yoghurt
1 tbsp nigella seeds
1 red chilli, finely chopped
   (deseed if you just want the
   flavour and not the heat)

bunch of freshly chopped
   mint leaves
2 large aubergines
1 tbsp extra virgin olive oil
1 tsp fennel seeds

• • • ·· • • • ·· • • • ·· • • • ·· • • • ·· • • • ·· • • • ·· • • •

To make the labneh, mix the salt into the yoghurt – you can do this in the yoghurt tub to save on washing up. Take a piece of clean muslin and spoon the yoghurt into the centre of it. Gather the muslin and tie it up, then hang it over a bowl and place in the fridge. You then need to leave this for 12 hours to allow the whey (liquid) to separate from the yoghurt.

After 12 hours, turn out the labneh into a clean bowl (discard the whey) and mix through the nigella seeds, chilli and mint. Set aside in the fridge while you roast the aubergines.

Preheat the oven to 200°C/gas 6.

Slice the aubergines in half lengthways and rub all over with the oil, then sprinkle with the fennel seeds. Place on a baking tray, cut side up. Bake in the preheated oven for 15 minutes until the aubergine flesh begins to collapse and the skin starts to blacken and burst.

Serve the warm roasted aubergines with the labneh alongside. Garnish with a little extra chilli, mint and nigella seeds, if you like.

Ful Medames STEWED FAVA BEANS

When I was at university my friend introduced me to the most moreish of brunches, which I remember vividly to this day. A meze style of brunch items were selected from his time growing up in the Middle East. It included merguez-like sausages, large stems of parsley, hummus and then this beautiful dish called *ful medames*, comprising mashed fava beans, topped off with Arabic-style bread such as khobez; so lovely and light. Typically this is made from dried fava beans, which we all know as broad beans, but if you can't get hold of these, pre-soaked tinned broad beans work equally well – I use these in the recipe.

SERVES 3

PER SERVING:
CALORIES 125KCAL
FAT 4G
SUGAR 1G

1 x 400g tin broad beans, drained and rinsed
pinch of salt, or to taste
1 garlic clove, crushed
juice of ½ lemon

1 tbsp olive oil
1 tsp ground cumin
freshly chopped parsley, to garnish (optional)

Place the broad beans in a bowl, then using the back of a fork, crush them to a coarse paste.

Season with the salt, then add all the other ingredients (except the garnish) and mix until thoroughly combined.

Sprinkle the top with some parsley, if you like, then serve with khobez bread.

Huevos Rancheros MEXICAN BAKED EGGS

This is a Mexican-inspired brunch dish that combines lots of healthy ingredients such as eggs, beans and tomatoes, plus a spicy kick from green chilli. It's a perfect pick-me-up that is well-balanced and particularly good on a grey morning. It's typically served with queso fresco, a Mexican crumbly cheese, but I've substituted a sprinkling of salty feta as it's easier to get hold of.

SERVES 2

PER SERVING:
CALORIES 257KCAL
FAT 10G
SUGAR 6G

2 eggs
1 soft flour tortilla
2 tsp freshly chopped coriander
20g feta, crumbled

FOR THE SALSA
1 tsp olive oil
½ large Spanish onion, finely chopped
2 tomatoes, finely chopped
2 green chillies, finely chopped
⅓ x 400g tin black beans, drained and rinsed
1 tsp ground cumin
salt and freshly ground black pepper

• • • ·· • • • ·· • • • ·· • • • ·· • • • ·· • • • ·· • • • ·· • • • ·· • • •

To make the salsa, heat the oil in a frying pan over a medium heat. Add the onion, tomatoes, chillies, beans, cumin and seasoning and cook for around 3 minutes until just warmed through and the tomatoes start to soften. Remove from the pan to a bowl and set aside.

Crack the eggs into the same pan and cook, sunny side up, for around 3 minutes, or until cooked to your liking (the eggs will cook in the juices and residual oil left in the pan).

Meanwhile, warm the tortilla – the easiest way to do this is to simply ping it in the microwave oven for 10 seconds on High (or follow the packet instructions).

To serve, lay the warm tortilla on a plate and spoon the salsa over. Carefully place the eggs on top, then scatter over the coriander and feta. Cut into two portions ready for sharing, and serve.

Sweetcorn, Feta and Cumin Fritters

I made this during my first audition for *This Morning*. It was the first time I'd ever had to cook to camera and I was so scared! I remember coming up with this recipe thinking it would be easy to prepare and quick to cook, and would look delicious on TV – and of course, taste great, too. I didn't want to over-complicate the recipe in case I forgot what to do when the camera was pointing in my face! This recipe was actually born out of a fridge full of leftovers. I love using up all my ingredients in the fridge and hate waste. I remember I had a bowl of sweetcorn and some feta left over, so I thought this would be the perfect little snack for brunch.

MAKES 12
(SERVE 3 PER PERSON)

PER SERVING:
CALORIES 268KCAL
FAT 10G
SUGAR 8G

FOR THE FRITTERS
100g feta, crumbled
½ x 198g tin sweetcorn
   kernels, drained
2 tbsp freshly chopped coriander
1 garlic clove, grated
150g chickpea flour
1 egg
2 tsp cumin seeds
1 tsp smoked paprika
salt and freshly ground
   black pepper

FOR THE DRESSING
100g low-fat natural yoghurt
2 tsp mint sauce
1 tsp ground cumin
freshly squeezed lemon juice,
   to taste

Put all the fritter ingredients into a bowl with about 175ml cold water and mix together – you want to create a batter of dropping consistency.

Heat a flat frying pan or griddle without oil over a medium to high heat for a couple of minutes. Once the pan is hot, for each fritter, drop a tablespoon of the batter into the pan and leave to cook for 2 minutes, then flip over and cook for a further 2 minutes until golden brown on both sides (cook as many fritters as you can fit into the pan at one time). Remove the cooked fritters to a plate and keep warm while you cook the rest (12 in total).

Meanwhile, mix all the dressing ingredients together in a small bowl. Season to taste with salt.

Drizzle the dressing over the warm fritters and serve immediately, accompanied by lots of fresh salad leaves and sliced tomatoes.

Punjabi Chole PUNJABI-STYLE CHICKPEAS

Traditionally, Punjabi chole (a dish of spicy chickpeas) is made using bread, and is sometimes served alongside a refreshing cold lassi (a yoghurt-based drink). This is a really simple, healthy and easy brunch that you can cook in advance, and the flavour just develops over time. I always have tinned chickpeas in the cupboard, so this is something I like to knock up quite often as it's so quick. This low-fat recipe provides fibre and protein to keep you feeling full.

SERVES 4

PER SERVING:
CALORIES 144KCAL
FAT 5G
SUGAR 5G

1 tbsp vegetable oil
1 large onion, finely chopped
3 garlic cloves, grated
5cm piece of fresh root ginger, peeled and grated
2 green chillies, split in half lengthways
1 cinnamon stick

2 tomatoes, finely diced
1 tsp garam masala
1 tsp ground turmeric
1 x 400g tin chickpeas, drained and rinsed
2 tbsp roughly chopped coriander
salt

Heat the oil in a large pan over a medium heat, add the onion and leave to cook for about 10 minutes, or until the onion is softened and beginning to colour.

Stir in the garlic, ginger, chillies and cinnamon stick and cook for 3 minutes. Add the tomatoes, garam masala and turmeric and cook for 2–3 minutes, then add 200ml cold water along with the chickpeas. Bring to a simmer and cook for a further 5 minutes.

Remove from the heat and discard the cinnamon stick. Season to taste with salt, stir in the coriander and serve warm with wholemeal pitta.

Grilled Herrings with Kaffir and Chilli

Herring is such a delicious fish. I don't tend to cook it very often, but when I do I always wonder why I don't use it more often. Herring is naturally oily and high in omega-3 fatty acids, which makes this a healthy and vibrant brunch. The kaffir lime leaves lift this whole dish, but if you're struggling to get hold of them then you can use some lime peel and add it in the same way.

SERVES 4

PER SERVING:
CALORIES 457KCAL
FAT 32G
SUGAR NONE

4 x 225g whole herrings, gutted and scales removed
1 tbsp coconut oil
1 garlic clove, finely sliced
2.5cm piece of fresh root ginger, peeled and cut into thin matchsticks (julienned)

3 red chillies, split in half lengthways
6 kaffir lime leaves
pinch of ground turmeric
pinch of salt

• •

Preheat the grill to high.

Thoroughly wash the herrings to make sure all the loose scales are removed, then pat them dry.

Rub the herrings all over with the oil, then stuff the insides with the garlic. Place on the rack in a grill pan, put the ginger, chillies and lime leaves on or around the herrings and sprinkle over the turmeric and salt.

Grill for about 8–10 minutes, or until the skin is crispy and the fish are cooked all the way through. Serve immediately.

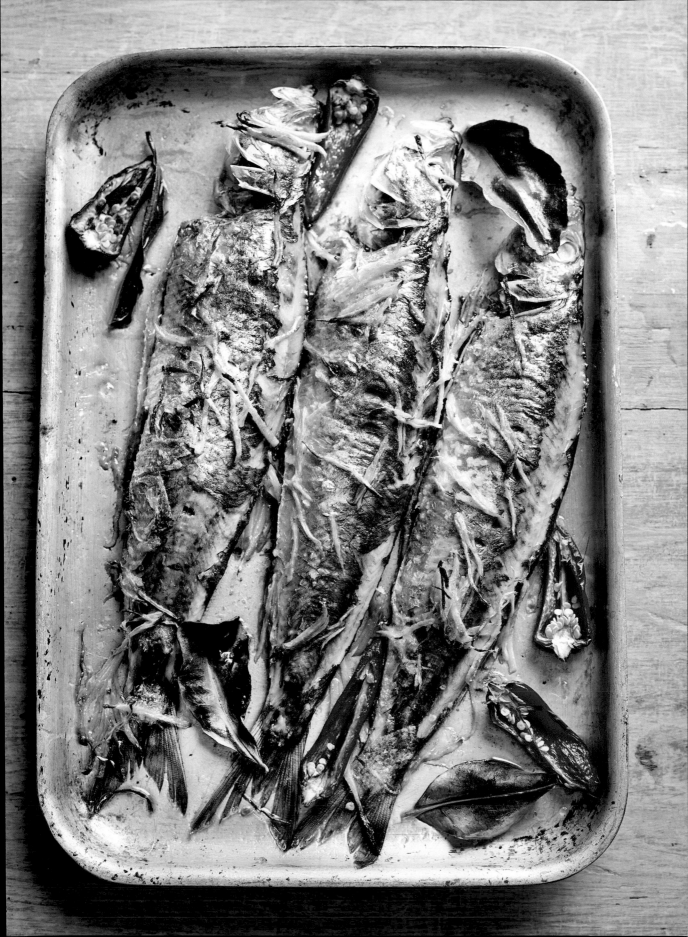

Beet and Ginger Smoothie

This is an energising smoothie bursting with antioxidant goodness that's perfect for breakfast when you just don't have the time to prepare much. You can blitz this up and take it on the road with you, or even make it the night before if you know you have a lot on in the morning.

SERVES 2

PER SERVING:
CALORIES 127KCAL
FAT 1G
SUGAR 24G

2 carrots (peel left on), washed
½ cantaloupe melon, peeled, seeded and cut into chunks
2 cold cooked beetroot (not in vinegar)

5cm piece of fresh root ginger (peel on), washed
juice of 1 lemon

• •

Place all the ingredients in a blender or food processor and blitz until you have a thick smoothie.

Pour into a glass or glasses and either drink immediately or chill in the fridge overnight and serve the next day. If serving the next day, give the smoothie a quick stir before drinking.

Fresh Coconut Milk with Cinnamon and Bitter Chocolate

Making your own coconut milk at home is so rewarding. I think a lot of people don't understand how it's made, or think it's the water inside the coconut that makes the milk – but that's just coconut water and nothing else. To make coconut milk it's actually the flesh you need in order to create this delicious dairy-free milk alternative. To make it at home is easy, all you need is some coconuts, some water and a food processor (you can make it by hand but it'll obviously take a bit longer and will require some elbow grease!). You'll also need some muslin for straining the liquid (see the photographs overleaf).

SERVES 4

PER SERVING:
CALORIES 626KCAL
FAT 58G
SUGAR 11G

2 brown coconuts
about 700ml hot water
3 tbsp good-quality unsweetened dark/ bitter cocoa powder
1 tsp ground cinnamon, or to taste
1 tsp good-quality vanilla extract
about 4 cinnamon sticks, to serve
1 tbsp agave syrup (optional)

• • • • ·· • • • • · · • • • · · • • • · · • • • ·· • • • · · • • • • •

Pierce the 'eyes' of each coconut using the tip of a sharp knife and then drain off and discard the water from inside.

One at a time, wrap each coconut in a kitchen towel and using a rolling pin, crack it into pieces. Carefully remove the coconut flesh from the hairy skin, then remove any brown bits with a sharp knife.

Once you have cracked both coconuts, place all the white pieces of flesh into a food processor along with the hot water and blitz until smooth.

Place a piece of clean muslin over a large jug and carefully pour the blitzed mixture into the muslin to strain out any solid bits of coconut, then squeeze the mixture to extract as much liquid as possible.

Rinse out the food processor and return the strained coconut milk to it along with the cocoa powder, ground cinnamon and vanilla extract. Blitz until fully combined. Taste and add the agave syrup for extra sweetness, if needed. Pour into a jug and chill before serving.

Stir well before serving. Serve in glasses with a stick of cinnamon in each glass as a stirrer.

Aloo Paratha SPICY POTATO BREAD

I remember when I was at university after a long night of partying, waking up to the smell of aloo paratha cooked by a friend's mum – the smell was truly intoxicating, with the combination of spices, chilli and coriander and the freshly cooked Indian-style bread. The thought alone literally makes me salivate! Traditionally this is made with oodles of butter or ghee, but I'd like to share with you a recipe that does away with all that butter and guilt.

MAKES 8

PER BREAD:
CALORIES 205KCAL
FAT 4G
SUGAR 1G

FOR THE 'ALOO' (POTATOES)
2 medium potatoes, unpeeled
2 garlic cloves, finely chopped
2.5cm piece of fresh root ginger, peeled and grated
1 tbsp mild madras curry powder
2 green chillies, finely chopped
2–3 tbsp freshly chopped coriander
salt

FOR THE PARATHA
300g plain flour, plus extra for dusting
1 tbsp cumin seeds
½ tsp salt
150–180ml warm water
about 2 tbsp vegetable oil

• • • • • • • • • • • • • • • • • • • • • • • • • • • • • • • • • • • • • • • • • • • • • • •

To start the 'aloo', cook the whole potatoes in their skins in a pan of boiling water for about 10 minutes, or until the skins start to split a bit. Drain well and leave to cool.

Meanwhile, to make the paratha, mix the flour, cumin seeds and salt in a large mixing bowl. Add the warm water, then using a wooden spoon, mix together to make a soft, pliable dough (you may need more or less water depending on the type of flour you are using). Form the dough into a ball, then cover with a damp cloth and leave to rest at room temperature for 20 minutes.

In the meantime, finish preparing the 'aloo'. Once the potatoes are cool, peel then mash them in a bowl with all the remaining 'aloo' ingredients until the mixture resembles a spicy mashed potato mixture.

Divide the paratha dough into 8 even pieces, then shape each one into a slightly flattened ball – each should be about the size of a satsuma. Take one ball of dough and create a small cavity in the centre, add a spoonful of the

Recipe continues overleaf

Aloo Paratha *continued*

potato mixture in the cavity and then carefully mould the dough around to enclose the filling completely. Repeat to make 8 paratha.

Carefully dust the work surface with flour, then roll out each stuffed ball of dough to a circle about 5mm thickness – don't worry if the potato mixture comes through the dough, this is perfectly normal.

Heat a frying pan over a really high heat and then carefully brush the surface of the hot pan with a little oil. Add one paratha to the pan and cook until you see bubbles on the surface of the dough and the dough starts to rise (this will take less than a minute). Turn the paratha over and cook the other side in the same way, then transfer to a plate and keep warm.

Repeat this process, brushing the pan with oil and cooking one paratha at a time, until they are all cooked. Serve the parathas warm.

These paratha are delicious served with my refreshing Raita with Pomegranate and Mint (see page 213).

Baked Moroccan Eggs

These Moroccan-style eggs are so easy to cook, as well as being vibrant and colourful, and are perfect if you have friends popping over unexpectedly. This dish delivers real wow factor and is heady with spice, so it delivers a great flavour punch too. Warm Arabic-style khobez bread or toasted wholemeal pitta is the perfect complement.

SERVES 4

PER SERVING:
CALORIES 145KCAL
FAT 9G
SUGAR 5G

1 tbsp olive oil
½ Spanish onion, grated
2 garlic cloves, grated
1 tsp paprika
1 tsp ground cumin
1 tsp ground coriander

3 large tomatoes, thinly sliced
2 tbsp freshly chopped coriander, plus extra to garnish
4 eggs
salt and freshly ground black pepper

Preheat the oven to 200°C/gas 6.

Pour the oil over the base of a large, ovenproof skillet or heavy-based frying pan, then scatter the onion, garlic, spices and some salt and pepper over. Layer the tomato slices over the top until they have all been used up, then scatter over the chopped coriander. Crack the eggs into the skillet on top of the tomatoes.

Bake in the preheated oven for 15 minutes, or until the eggs are just cooked with soft yolks. Serve garnished with a little more coriander if you like.

LUNCHTIME INSPIRATION

'Colour is as important as taste – you eat with your eyes, too – so cook with a range of ingredients that make the plate look vibrant and appealing.'

LUNCHTIME INSPIRATION

I find that when I am trying to eat better and more healthily there are a few things that I can struggle with. Lunchtime, in my opinion, is the hardest meal of the day, and whether you are working from home, working in the office, looking after the kids or just out and about, it's so hard to get a balanced lunch that makes you feel full and satisfied.

I think that if you try to get through the day with only celery and carrot sticks for lunch you'll be setting yourself up for failure. To enjoy a healthy and balanced lunch you need to apply the same thought as you would to dinner, but make it speedier. Also, you don't want to scrimp on flavour and you need to choose foods that will give the feeling of fullness, as well as hitting all those taste buds in your mouth.

So with a little bit of planning and some imagination, these recipes will make you feel full, happy and satisfied, and you'll be eating something that tastes like a meal. Lunch is also often quicker to prepare than you might imagine, plus it will ideally provide you with essential nutrients you need to get on with the rest of the day.

Most of the recipes in this chapter are pretty quick to prepare, and I'm sure that once you've mastered them they'll become part of your regular lunchtime repertoire.

Chicken and Green Mango Salad

This salad is fuss-free and packed full of flavour and goodness. The green mango has a sour-and-sweet taste and brings this salad to a different level of flavour. You can use leftover roast chicken or you can bake some fresh chicken for this salad.

SERVES 4

PER SERVING:
CALORIES 296KCAL
FAT 11G
SUGAR 13G

100g reduced-fat crème fraîche
1 tsp palm sugar
1 red chilli, seeded and finely chopped, plus extra to garnish
juice of 2 limes
½ head white cabbage, cored and shredded
1 green mango, peeled, stoned and shredded or cut into matchsticks (julienned)

40g shelled pistachios, toasted and crushed
handful of freshly torn mint leaves, plus extra to garnish
2 cold cooked skinless and boneless chicken breast fillets, sliced
salt and freshly ground black pepper

· ·

In a large bowl, mix together the crème fraîche, palm sugar, chilli, lime juice and seasoning until they are completely combined.

Toss all the remaining ingredients (except the chicken) into the dressing.

Serve the salad with the sliced chicken over the top, and garnish with some extra chilli and mint.

Broad Bean, Mint and Fennel 'Hummus'

Broad beans are nutty and a little bitter in flavour, and they work well when paired with mint. This is a delicious, low-fat alternative to hummus and perfect for dipping, or you can pack it in a lunchbox and serve with some vegetable crudités, pitta bread and feta for a healthy balanced lunch.

SERVES 2

PER SERVING:
CALORIES 273KCAL
FAT 3G
SUGAR 10G

250g frozen peas
250g frozen baby broad beans
1 tbsp fennel seeds, lightly toasted (see page 17)
125g fat-free natural yoghurt
2 tbsp fresh lemon juice
leaves from 10 sprigs of mint
2 tbsp freshly snipped chives
salt and freshly ground black pepper

• • • ·· ·· • • • ·· ·· • • • ·· ·· • • • ·· ·· • • • ·· ·· • • • ·· ·· • • •

Put the peas and broad beans into a bowl and pour over boiling water from the kettle to cover. Leave to stand for a few minutes until defrosted, then drain.

Using a pestle and mortar, lightly crush the fennel seeds.

Drain the defrosted peas and beans, put them in a food processor along with the crushed fennel seeds and all the remaining ingredients, and pulse to create a hummus-like texture.

Adjust the seasoning to taste and serve. You can also serve this spread on crostini (grilled day-old bread rubbed with a little garlic).

Spicy Chilled Gazpacho

Traditionally an Andalusian peasant dish, this cold tomato soup shouts summer to me and I love making it on hot days as it's so cooling and refreshing. Some people like to serve gazpacho with ice cubes, but I think if you chill it well in advance, you don't then need to add the ice as it'll only dilute the flavours. I've made this dish thicker in texture than a classic gazpacho so that you to feel fuller and more satisfied once you've eaten it.

SERVES 6

PER SERVING:
CALORIES 151KCAL
FAT 1G
SUGAR 9G

800g mixed ripe tomatoes
1 red onion, roughly chopped
1 red pepper, seeded and cored
½ cucumber, peeled and seeded
1 garlic clove, peeled
1 red chilli (including seeds)
1 tsp smoked paprika
1 tsp ground coriander
150g fresh breadcrumbs
100ml passata
3 tbsp red wine or sherry vinegar, or to taste
salt and freshly ground black pepper
freshly chopped dill and mint leaves, to garnish

Place all the ingredients (except the vinegar, seasoning and herb garnish) in a food processor and pulse until combined and relatively smooth.

Transfer to a bowl, cover with clingfilm and chill in the fridge for at least 1 hour and up to 4 hours.

Before serving, season the gazpacho with the vinegar and salt and pepper to taste. Serve in bowls, garnished with the chopped dill and mint.

Salmon Ceviche with Orange Segments, Lime and Fennel

Ceviche (cured raw fish) is a common dish across South America, with a number of variations in the preparation and the flavour, but all of them share the same quality of using the freshest fish you can get your hands on. Ceviche isn't something that people like to prepare at home very often, out of fear I think, but I have to reassure you that it is so easy to make. The most important thing is to make sure you buy the freshest fish possible (ask your fishmonger), then it's really one of the most simple and delicious dishes to prepare.

SERVES 4

PER SERVING:
CALORIES 224KCAL
FAT 12G
SUGAR 10G

FOR THE CEVICHE
300g good-quality fresh
   skinless and boneless
   salmon fillet, trimmed
1 tbsp lime zest
juice of 5 limes
1 tbsp unrefined light
   muscovado sugar
pinch of salt

FOR THE SALAD
1 tbsp wholegrain French
   mustard
1 tbsp olive oil
juice of 1 lemon
1 medium fennel bulb,
   thinly sliced
1 medium orange, segmented
   (skin and membranes
   removed)
100g mixed lettuce leaves
handful of coarsely chopped
   parsley
salt and freshly ground
   black pepper

• •

To make the ceviche, cut the salmon into slices of 2–3mm thickness. Place the slices on a platter, then sprinkle with the lime zest, lime juice, sugar and salt. Cover with clingfilm and chill in the fridge for 20 minutes.

To make the salad, in a serving bowl, mix together the mustard, oil, lemon juice and seasoning until emulsified, then toss through the fennel, orange segments, lettuce leaves and parsley.

Arrange the salmon ceviche on top of the salad and serve.

Chicken Laab

Laab is a Thai salad usually made with minced pork that is tenderised using a heavy cleaver (you bash away relentlessly at the meat to create fresh minced meat – it is more tender and flavourful than the pre-minced kind you find in the supermarket). Making your own minced meat from scratch is easy, and here I use chicken instead of pork to keep the fat content low.

All you need to do is to place skinless and boneless chicken breast fillets in a food processor and blitz until you achieve a minced consistency. I prefer to make mince myself so that I can also monitor the amount of fat that goes into the meal.

SERVES 4

PER SERVING:
CALORIES 290KCAL
FAT 7G
SUGAR 6G

50g rice (basmati works best here)
2 garlic cloves, grated
2 red or green bird's eye chillies, seeded and finely chopped (leave seeds in if you like the heat)
handful of fresh coriander (roughly chop the stalks and finely chop the leaves)
2 tbsp vegetable oil
2 shallots, finely chopped

600g minced chicken
1 tbsp shrimp paste
2 tbsp fish sauce
juice of 2 limes
1 tbsp unrefined dark muscovado sugar
10 mint leaves, finely chopped
chopped spring onions, to garnish
lettuce 'cups', to serve (Little Gem or iceberg lettuce both work well)

Heat a wok over a high heat until hot, add the rice and dry-fry for around 3 minutes until it has browned, shaking the pan a bit every now and then. Remove from the heat and lightly pound the rice using a pestle and mortar, then set aside for the garnish.

Using the same pestle and mortar, lightly pound together the prepared garlic, chillies and coriander stalks to make a rough paste.

Heat the oil in the same wok over a high heat, add the shallots and the paste and stir-fry for 3 minutes. Add the minced chicken and stir-fry for about 5 minutes until the chicken is cooked through and browned slightly. Add the shrimp paste, fish sauce, lime juice and sugar and stir-fry for a further 2–3 minutes.

Remove from the heat and toss through the chopped coriander and mint leaves. Garnish with spring onions and the toasted rice and serve in lettuce cups.

Baked Tofu with Sriracha

Tofu, also known as bean curd, can be found in most supermarkets. The process of creating tofu is achieved by pressing soy milk into solid blocks, and it is available in a variety of consistencies, from firm to soft set (silken). Tofu is subtle in flavour and light to eat, therefore it takes on the strong flavour of the sriracha spicy sauce really well in this recipe. It's also low in fat and high in protein. Baking tofu before cooking is so simple, yet the process changes the texture of the tofu and enables you to cook with it easily without it breaking up when you are stir-frying or adding it to other dishes.

SERVES 4

PER SERVING:
CALORIES 156KCAL
FAT 7G
SUGAR 5G

1 x 396g packet original tofu, drained
1 tsp vegetable oil
3 garlic cloves, finely chopped
5cm piece of fresh root ginger, peeled and cut into thin matchsticks (julienned)
2 tbsp finely chopped coriander stalks
3 tbsp Sriracha (see page 219)
1 tbsp light soy sauce
½ tsp freshly ground Sichuan pepper
pinch of white pepper
½ red onion, sliced
½ red pepper, seeded and sliced or chopped
100g frozen peas
freshly squeezed lime juice, to taste
freshly chopped coriander leaves, to garnish

• •

Preheat the oven to 200°C/gas 6.

Chop the tofu into 2cm squares and place on a baking tray. Bake in the preheated oven for around 35 minutes. This will dry out the tofu and ensure it doesn't break up when it is stir-fried. Remove from the oven and set aside.

Heat the oil in a wok over a medium to high heat, add the garlic, ginger and coriander stalks and stir-fry for around 3 minutes until fragrant.

Add the sriracha and soy sauce, followed by the Sichuan pepper, white pepper, red onion, red pepper and tofu, and stir-fry for around 3 minutes. Add the peas and stir-fry for a further 2 minutes.

Squeeze over the lime juice, garnish with coriander leaves and serve.

Butterflied Harissa Sardines

Sardines are packed full of flavour, their naturally oily flesh is high in healthy fats and they are rich in protein, but the biggest bonus is that they are sustainable, cheap and easy to get hold of. Because sardines are so rich in flavour, they can really withstand the punchy flavours of the fiery harissa. This is perfect served with Kale and Sumac Tabbouleh (see page 66). See the following pages for recipe photos.

SERVES 5

PER SERVING:
CALORIES 368KCAL
FAT 22G
SUGAR NONE

10 fresh sardines, gutted, scaled and butterflied

FOR THE MARINADE
4 tbsp freshly chopped parsley
2 tbsp freshly chopped coriander
zest of 1 lemon
2 tbsp fresh lemon juice
1 tbsp home-made Harissa (see page 212)
2 garlic cloves, finely chopped
1 tbsp rapeseed oil
1 tsp pink peppercorns, crushed
salt, to taste

• •

Preheat the grill to high.

Lay the prepared sardines skin-side up in a single layer on a baking sheet.

Mix together all the marinade ingredients in a bowl, then spoon this mixture evenly over the sardines making sure they are all completely covered.

Grill for about 5 minutes, or until the sardines are completely cooked through. Serve immediately with Kale and Sumac Tabbouleh (see page 66) or wholemeal bread and fresh salad leaves.

Mauritian Sardine Salad

This is one of my favourite go-to light lunches. It is a typical Mauritian dish we used to have when we got back from school, served with crackers and lemon juice. I love the strong flavour of the sardines, but this recipe works equally well with smoked mackerel – and both are rich in healthy omega-3 fats.

SERVES 1

PER SERVING:
CALORIES 288KCAL
FAT 15G
SUGAR 9G

1 x 100g tin grilled sardines
½ red onion, finely sliced
2 plum tomatoes, roughly chopped
1 green chilli, seeded and finely chopped
½ lemon (with skin on), finely sliced
1 tbsp red wine vinegar
1 tbsp freshly chopped parsley
salt and freshly ground black pepper

Place all the ingredients in a bowl and mix together gently until combined. Adjust the seasoning to taste.

Serve with rye crispbread or wholegrain crackers if you like.

Grilled Prawns with Apple and Ginger Coleslaw

This unusual combination of fruit and seafood works really well, and the sweetness of the prawns with the sharpness of the apple creates such a unique taste sensation. The whole point about tasty food is the mouth feel – food that hits all the taste buds on your tongue makes you feel full and leaves you satisfied.

SERVES 4

PER SERVING:
CALORIES 155KCAL
FAT 4G
SUGAR 10G

300g (prepared weight) raw king prawns, shelled and deveined
3 tsp Chinese five-spice powder
1 tbsp sesame oil
½ head Chinese cabbage, thinly sliced
1 large carrot, peeled and cut into matchsticks (julienned)
1 red-skinned eating apple, cored and cut into matchsticks (julienned)
3 spring onions, finely chopped
150g beansprouts
handful of freshly chopped coriander

FOR THE DRESSING
7.5cm piece of fresh root ginger, peeled and grated
juice of 2–3 limes
1 tsp unrefined light muscovado sugar
2 tbsp light soy sauce

Preheat the grill to high.

In a bowl, mix together the prawns, five-spice powder and sesame oil. Arrange the prawns in a single layer on a baking tray. Grill for 5–7 minutes until they are charred and cooked all the way through.

Meanwhile, whisk together all the dressing ingredients in a mixing bowl until completely combined and the sugar has dissolved. Add the cabbage, carrot, apple, spring onions, beansprouts and coriander and toss to mix.

Serve the coleslaw with the grilled prawns alongside or on top.

Wasabi Cured Salmon

Curing is a method of preserving raw meats and fish, and it works very well with salmon. Wasabi is also known as Japanese horseradish and it has a hot and fiery character, very similar to English mustard. It adds a wonderful depth to this cured salmon. This recipe is a make-ahead dish, and once the salmon is cured it will keep in the fridge for up to a week.

SERVES 10

PER SERVING:
CALORIES 180KCAL
FAT 11G
SUGAR NONE

500g coarse salt
500g unrefined caster sugar
1 tbsp coriander seeds
1 tbsp fennel seeds
1 tbsp black peppercorns
2 tbsp wasabi paste

4 tbsp sake (rice wine)
1kg boneless side of salmon (or use boneless fillets if they are easier to get hold of), skin removed

Place the salt, sugar, coriander seeds, fennel seeds and black peppercorns in a food processor and blitz until very smooth.

In a mug, whisk together the wasabi paste and sake, then rub this into the salmon all over.

Place the salmon in a glass or non-metallic dish (in a single layer if using fillets) and spread the salt mixture over the top, pressing it firmly into the fish. Cover and chill in the fridge for 48 hours.

After the salmon has cured, rinse the salt mixture off and dry the fish using kitchen towels. At this stage the cured salmon can be kept in a covered container in the fridge for up to a week, if you like.

To serve, slice the salmon very thinly and serve with reduced-fat crème fraîche, Blackened Sweetcorn Salsa (see page 170) and toasted dark rye bread.

Som Tam GREEN PAPAYA SALAD

In my opinion, this has to be the number one Thai street food dish. Som tam salad epitomises the cuisine of the country by exciting all the taste buds – Thai food is renowned for its perfect balance of hot, sour, sweet and salty and this salad is exactly that. I find that the hardest thing when eating healthily is to think of food that delivers on both taste and satisfaction, and for me, som tam does just that. If you struggle to find an unripe papaya, you can replace it with a mixture of courgette and carrot. This recipe comes from the cookery school in Chang Mai where I learned how to make som tam the local way.

SERVES 6

PER SERVING:
CALORIES 182KCAL
FAT 6G
SUGAR 10G

3 tbsp fish sauce
2 tbsp unrefined light muscovado sugar
1 tbsp shrimp paste
juice of 2 limes
4 garlic cloves, peeled
4 red chillies, seeded
2 tbsp freshly chopped coriander stalks
1 green papaya

1 carrot, peeled
100g beansprouts
6 cherry tomatoes, cut in half
large handful of freshly chopped coriander leaves
200g cooked brown shrimps
large handful of freshly torn basil leaves
75g unsalted peanuts, toasted, to garnish

Using a pestle and mortar, pound together the fish sauce, sugar, shrimp paste, lime juice, garlic, chillies and coriander stalks until you get a sauce/dressing that is sweet, salty, sour and hot. You might want to add more lime juice, sugar, fish sauce or chillies, according to taste. Set aside.

Slice the green papaya in half lengthways and crack it open. Scrape out the seeds and discard. Turn over each half and peel off the green skin. Cut the papaya and carrot into thin matchsticks (julienne) or coarsely grate.

Combine the papaya and carrot with all the remaining ingredients in a large bowl, reserving half of the basil and all the peanuts for garnishing. Pour over the sauce/dressing and toss to mix.

Garnish with the toasted peanuts and remaining basil, then serve.

Steamed Hake with Wasabi, Soy and Ginger

I first tasted this dish at a friend's house; she had just had her second baby and is a busy mum with not much time. I popped over to her house unexpectedly and she created this dish for me in no time at all. It's so simple, as you place everything into foil and then let the oven work its magic and steam the fish to perfection. I use hake in this dish, but you could also use cod fillets or any other firm white fish of your choice.

SERVES 1

PER SERVING:
CALORIES 182KCAL
FAT 4G
SUGAR 1G

1 skinless and boneless
   hake fillet
juice of ½ lemon
1 tsp wasabi paste
1 tbsp light soy sauce
2.5cm piece of fresh root ginger,
   peeled and finely shredded
freshly ground black pepper,
   to taste

TO GARNISH (OPTIONAL)
½ large red chilli, finely sliced
2–3 spring onions, finely sliced

• •

Preheat the oven to 200°C/gas 6.

Take a large piece of foil and place the hake in the middle of it, then add all the remaining ingredients (except the garnishes), placing them on top of the fish.

Loosely close the foil around the fish to make a sealed parcel, giving the fish room to steam inside. Place on a baking sheet. Bake in the preheated oven for 15 minutes until cooked all the way through.

Garnish with the chilli and spring onions, if you like. Serve with some steamed green beans or mangetout.

Flaked Mackerel with Lemon and Fennel

This stunningly simple recipe takes less than 10 minutes to prepare. It's a really refreshing and robust salad, perfect served as a light meal for a get-together.

SERVES 4

PER SERVING:
CALORIES 328KCAL
FAT 27G
SUGAR 3G

4 smoked mackerel fillets
2 tbsp white wine vinegar
2 tbsp Dijon mustard
1 tbsp rapeseed oil
150g baby salad leaves,
    or iceberg lettuce,
    thinly shredded

1 lemon, thinly sliced using
    a mandolin
1 small fennel bulb, thinly
    sliced using a mandolin
handful of freshly chopped dill
handful of (drained) capers,
    coarsely chopped

• • • • ·· • ·· • • ·· • • • ·· • • ·· • • • ·· • • • ·· • • • ·· • • • ·· • • • ·· • •

Take the mackerel fillets and peel away and discard the skin. Flake the mackerel flesh and leave to one side.

Put the vinegar, mustard and oil into a clean jam jar and give it a good shake until the dressing is emulsified.

Put all the remaining ingredients into a bowl along with the flaked mackerel and mix carefully by hand. Drizzle over the dressing, toss gently to mix and serve.

Kale and Sumac Tabbouleh

This Levantine salad is usually made with more herbs than bulgar wheat, but here I've also added kale as I love this bitter-tasting green and it brings another dimension to a traditional dish. This tabbouleh, with its inclusion of the tangy, lemony sumac spice, works perfectly served with grilled fish or seafood and is particularly good with my Baked Sea Bass with Pink Peppercorns (see page 147).

SERVES 4

PER SERVING:
CALORIES 132KCAL
FAT 6G
SUGAR 3G

50g bulgar wheat
2 tbsp extra virgin olive oil
zest and juice of 1 lemon
bunch of finely chopped
    mint leaves
large bunch of freshly
    chopped parsley
½ tsp ground allspice
1 tsp ground sumac

50g kale, finely chopped
2 tomatoes, seeded and
    finely chopped
½ cucumber, peeled, seeded
    and finely chopped
salt, to taste
torn Romaine or cos lettuce
    leaves, to serve

• •

Place the bulgar wheat in a heatproof bowl and pour over enough boiling water to cover the wheat by 1cm. Stir, cover with clingfilm and set aside for 15 minutes until most of the water has been absorbed, then drain.

In a large bowl, whisk together the oil, lemon zest and juice, mint, parsley, ground spices and salt until the mixture has emulsified.

Toss through the soaked bulgar wheat and all the remaining ingredients (except the lettuce), then serve on a bed of torn lettuce leaves.

Black and Yellow Mustard Cauliflower

Cauliflower is the king of vegetables and, in my opinion, is one of those vegetables that has an almost meaty texture that leaves you feeling full. This dish is quite powerful in flavour and if left overnight it gets even stronger. I like to use the whole cauliflower and not waste one bit, so here I cut the cauliflower into small florets, cut the stalks into small pieces and finely slice the leaves. It's all edible and there's no need for waste; these are the lessons from my mum that, the older I get, I seem to be applying more and more.

SERVES 6

PER SERVING:
CALORIES 93KCAL
FAT 5G
SUGAR 3G

1 tbsp mustard oil
2 tbsp yellow mustard seeds
2 tbsp black mustard seeds
a large handful of fresh curry leaves
1 cauliflower, cut into small florets, plus stalks finely chopped and leaves finely sliced

3 green chillies, split in half lengthways
1 tsp ground turmeric
salt
freshly chopped coriander, to garnish

• •

Heat the oil in a large saucepan over a medium heat, add all the mustard seeds and the curry leaves and sauté until you hear the seeds pop. Add the cauliflower florets, stalks and leaves and sauté for a few minutes.

Add the chillies, turmeric and 400ml cold water to the pan, then bring to a simmer and cook, uncovered, for 20–25 minutes until the florets have softened. Stir occasionally during cooking, and add more water if the dish becomes too dry.

Season to taste with salt, garnish with coriander and serve hot.

Griddled Sweet Potatoes with Mint, Chilli and Smoked Garlic

Smoked garlic (see Note below) has a milder flavour than raw garlic and therefore adds a beautiful BBQ-style taste to dishes. Here the sweet potatoes, which are rich in antioxidants and a good source of fibre, are griddled to concentrate their sweetness and to create a charred caramel flavour (equally you could do this on a BBQ). The smoked garlic in this dish intensifies the flavour. This is perfect hot, warm or cold and makes a change from traditional baked sweet potatoes.

SERVES 3

PER SERVING:
CALORIES 272KCAL
FAT 10G
SUGAR 20G

2 large sweet potatoes, washed and sliced lengthways into 5mm-thick slices
olive oil, for brushing
salt

FOR THE DRESSING
2 smoked garlic cloves, finely chopped (see Note below)
handful of freshly chopped mint leaves
1 large red chilli, seeded and finely chopped
2 tbsp extra virgin olive oil
1 tbsp sherry vinegar

Brush the sweet potato slices with oil to coat them all over and season with salt.

Preheat a griddle pan over a high heat until smoking hot and then place the sweet potato slices straight into the pan (you may need to do this in batches). Griddle them for 3 minutes on each side until cooked, turning once. Using tongs, transfer the slices from the pan to a large platter.

In a small bowl, mix together all the dressing ingredients until completely combined. Season to taste with salt.

Pour the dressing over the griddled potato slices and serve warm.

NOTE
If you are struggling to get hold of smoked garlic, instead you can use a whole head of raw garlic – simply wrap it in foil and bake in a preheated oven at 160°C/gas 2½ for 30 minutes. This will mellow the flavour, and the baked garlic flesh can then be squeezed out of its skin directly into the dressing.

Endive and Pomegranate with Tahini Dressing

I love using endive in salads, particularly in starters as it has a wonderful bitterness that opens up the palate. The flavour of this salad is Persian-inspired, with the use of tahini (sesame seed paste), which is known to help reduce cholesterol, and pomegranate to add a fruity hit to the dish.

SERVES 3

PER SERVING:
CALORIES 156KCAL
FAT 11G
SUGAR 3G

seeds from ½ pomegranate
2 heads of mixed endive/
    chicory, trimmed and
    separated into leaves
½ red onion, thinly sliced
1 plum tomato, seeded and diced
handful of coarsely chopped
    parsley
handful of pumpkin seeds

FOR THE DRESSING
2 tbsp tahini
½ tsp paprika
½ tsp ground cumin
salt, to taste

• •

Pick out and discard any bitter white pith from the pomegranate seeds. Set the seeds aside.

Put the endive leaves, red onion, tomato and parsley in a bowl and toss gently to mix. Combine all the dressing ingredients in a mug with 5 tablespoons of cold water.

Drizzle the dressing over the salad and then scatter over the pomegranate seeds and pumpkin seeds. Serve.

Beetroot and Orange with Pimento

Pimento, also known as allspice, is used a lot in Levant (Eastern Mediterranean) cooking. This dish is inspired by my time in Cyprus, where I remember sitting on the beachside eating a fragrant orange salad that had orange blossom and spices running through it. It's always hard to re-create holiday food memories but this does transport me back to the scent of grilled fish, the smell of the sea and that distinct aroma of the wonderful allspice berry.

SERVES 4

PER SERVING:
CALORIES 110KCAL
FAT 6G
SUGAR 10G

2 medium oranges, peeled and sliced, plus juice of ½ orange
2 medium cooked beetroot (not in vinegar), cooled and quartered
salad bowlful of rocket leaves
large handful of freshly chopped coriander leaves
1 tbsp orange blossom water
2 tbsp olive oil
1 tsp ground allspice or pimento
salt

• •

Arrange the orange slices and beetroot quarters on top of the rocket and sprinkle over the coriander.

In a small bowl, combine the orange juice, orange blossom water, oil, pimento and salt to taste, then pour over the salad and serve.

Ghanaian Beans and Okra

At university I made a lot of friends, and in particular a lot of friends from West Africa. I was immediately drawn to the big flavours of palm oil, plantain and scotch bonnet, massive pots of *jollof* rice and stews, and stunning party food. West African food is definitely a love of mine and this dish is a great way to use an ingredient many people are put off by – okra, also known as lady's fingers or gumbo. When okra cooks it releases a sap which can be quite gloopy with a texture that can be off-putting to some, but don't worry as this dish partially cooks the okra yet still retains its texture. I think this is a really good way of introducing okra to those who may be a little bit wary of this vegetable.

SERVES 4

PER SERVING:
CALORIES 222KCAL
FAT 7G
SUGAR 7G

50g dried shrimp, rehydrated overnight (see below)
4 plum tomatoes
1 onion, peeled
2 garlic cloves, peeled
2 tbsp vegetable oil
1 tbsp dried thyme
1 tbsp mild madras curry powder
1 scotch bonnet chilli, left whole
1 x 400g tin black-eyed beans, drained and rinsed
15–20 fresh okra, sliced in half lengthways
salt
freshly chopped coriander, to garnish

To rehydrate the dried shrimp, place in a bowl and cover with cold water, then leave in the fridge overnight. The next day, drain off any excess liquid and reserve the rehydrated shrimp.

Put the tomatoes, onion, garlic and rehydrated shrimp in a food processor and blitz to make a purée.

Heat the oil in a large pan over a medium heat, add the purée and cook until it starts to bubble and become fragrant, around 3–4 minutes. Add the thyme, curry powder and whole scotch bonnet and cook for a further 1–2 minutes (add some water if the mixture becomes a bit dry).

Add the black-eyed beans and okra along with some salt to taste, then reduce the heat to low, cover and cook for 15 minutes, stirring occasionally.

Scatter with coriander to garnish and serve hot or cold.

Baked Tofu and Beansprout Spicy Salad

Tofu is high in protein, low in fat and a good source of calcium. This salad is easy to prepare and perfect for weekday work lunches. It's fantastic if you are looking for a light lunch option but don't want to scrimp on flavour, and the best thing is it's really easy to transport once you've put it all together.

SERVES 4

PER SERVING:
CALORIES 276KCAL
FAT 13G
SUGAR 16G

1 x 396g packet tofu, drained
80g unsalted peanuts
1 cucumber, seeded and grated
1 large carrot, peeled and cut
   into matchsticks (julienned)
200g beansprouts
2 green chillies, seeded and
   thinly sliced
1 garlic clove, crushed
   or finely chopped
juice of 2 limes
2 tbsp light soy sauce
2 tbsp runny honey
large handful of holy
   basil leaves

• • • • • · · · · · · • · · · · · · · • · · · • • · · · · • · · • · · · • • · · · · · • · · · • •

Preheat the oven to 200°C/gas 6.

Cut the tofu into 2cm squares and place on a baking tray. Bake in the preheated oven for around 35 minutes. This will dry out the tofu and ensure it doesn't break up in the salad. Remove from the oven and set aside.

Meanwhile, heat a frying pan until hot, add the peanuts and dry-roast for about 3 minutes until lightly browned all over, shaking the pan occasionally. Leave to cool, then coarsely crush using a pestle and mortar.

In a large salad bowl, combine the cucumber, carrot and beansprouts, then top with the warm baked tofu.

In a small bowl, mix together the chillies, garlic, lime juice, soy sauce and honey until completely combined, then pour over the salad.

Tear over the holy basil leaves, scatter with the roasted peanuts and serve.

Stir-fried Vegetables with Togarashi

Togarashi is a Japanese chilli powder that you can find in specialist shops. It comprises a combination of seven different dried, powdered spices including chilli. It's unique in flavour, so it would be hard to suggest an alternative if you can't get hold of it. However, you could replace the powder with the zest of ½ orange, plus hot chilli powder, sesame seeds and some Sichuan pepper, added according to taste. This dish is packed with a variety of vegetables so is a great way to boost your vitamin and mineral intake.

SERVES 4

PER SERVING:
CALORIES 186KCAL
FAT 5G
SUGAR 10G

100g dried shiitake mushrooms
1 tbsp vegetable oil
3 large red or green chillies,
    halved lengthways
200g green beans, cut in half
200g mangetout, cut in half
200g baby corn, cut in half

3 tbsp light soy sauce
1 tbsp runny honey
400ml hot vegetable stock
2 tbsp togarashi
handful of freshly torn
    basil leaves

• •

Soak the shiitake mushrooms in hot water for 30 minutes, then drain and slice.

Heat the oil in a wok over a medium to high heat, add the chillies, green beans, mangetout, baby corn and sliced mushrooms and sauté until the vegetables start to soften, around 5–7 minutes, stirring often.

Add the soy sauce, honey, stock and togarashi and simmer for a further 5 minutes.

Scatter with torn basil leaves and serve.

Caribbean Allspice Salad with Pumpkin and Black Beans

Whenever I use allspice it always reminds me of fragrant West Indian food such as pepper pot soup, curried goat or the classic jerk seasoning. In fact, allspice is sometimes described as Jamaica pepper. The wonderful thing about allspice/pimento is that it has a flavour reminiscent of a number of other spices including juniper, black peppercorns, nutmeg and cinnamon, so by adding a touch of it to your food you end up adding lots of wonderful aromatic layers. Allspice/pimento is also used heavily in Levant cooking, which you can find on pages 66 and 71 in salads inspired by the Middle East. This salad is packed with heaps of flavour and is high in fibre, antioxidants and vitamins, making it a good low-fat lunch that's sure to keep hunger under control!

SERVES 4

PER SERVING
(WITH BROWN RICE):
CALORIES 265KCAL
FAT 10G
SUGAR 8G

350g pumpkin, seeded (skin left on), chopped into 2cm cubes
1 tbsp olive oil
1 large red onion, finely chopped
½ scotch bonnet chilli, seeded and finely chopped
1 x 400g tin black beans, drained and rinsed
300g cold cooked brown or white rice
1 red pepper, seeded and cut into cubes
1 tbsp freshly snipped chives
1–2 spring onions, chopped

FOR THE DRESSING
leaves from 10 sprigs of thyme
juice of 2 limes
2 tbsp extra virgin olive oil
1 tsp ground allspice
salt, to taste

Add the pumpkin to a pan of boiling water and cook for 10 minutes, or until tender. Drain, rinse with cold water and set aside to cool.

Heat the oil in a large, flameproof casserole over a medium heat, add the red onion, scotch bonnet and cooked pumpkin and sauté until the pumpkin starts to brown and caramelise.

Remove from the heat and transfer to a large serving platter. Mix in the beans, rice, red pepper, chives and spring onions.

In a jug, mix together all the ingredients for the dressing until emulsified, then pour over the salad and serve.

ONE-POT
WONDERS

'Prepare as much as you can from scratch, including making dishes in advance if you know you have a busy week ahead.'

ONE-POT WONDERS

One-pot cooking gets a lot of flak from some for appearing lazy and perhaps not as thoughtful as other styles of cooking. I was brought up by a Mauritian mum, and she relied on one-pot cooking. Some of my fondest memories are of lifting the lid off a pot of stew, curry or biryani to unveil the magic that had gone on inside, all in one single pot.

One-pot recipes are perfect for weeknights or even lazy weekends. Make them ahead ready to eat during the week, or put them on to cook in the morning and you've got dinner ready for the evening. If you have a slow cooker you can prepare dishes in it but cooking times will vary according to the slow cooker you have.

The beauty of one-pot cooking isn't only that you have just the one pot to wash up, but it also enables all the ingredients and flavours to meld together, creating a dish that in some cases can become even better overnight.

One-pot cooking can be really helpful when you are eating healthily, because you can prepare recipes in advance so that you have something ready to reheat when you are tired and hungry, particularly after a busy day at work or looking after the kids. I find these are the moments when I'll eat something that isn't that good for me, so I try to be prepared with a one-pot in the fridge.

In this chapter you'll find a broad range of world-inspired one-pots that will help you to eat well, feel inspired and stay nourished.

Jungle Curry with Turkey and Vegetables

Jungle curry is a Northern Thai curry that has a powerful and robust flavour. It is traditionally made using wild meats like wild boar, or even more unusual forms of protein such as frog, plus a range of vegetables. Typically these curries don't contain coconut milk (as coconuts are rare in Northern Thai jungles) and are heavily flavoured with green peppercorns, lemon grass, chilli and galangal (a potent ginger).

SERVES 4

PER SERVING:
CALORIES 170KCAL
FAT 4G
SUGAR 10G

1 tbsp vegetable oil
200g skinless and boneless turkey breast, cut into 5cm pieces
300ml vegetable stock
1 aubergine, cut into 2cm cubes
50g baby corn, cut into small pieces
50g snake beans or French beans, cut into small pieces
50g frozen peas
handful of freshly torn basil leaves

FOR THE JUNGLE CURRY PASTE
10 dried red chillies, soaked in hot water and drained (see page 17)
6 garlic cloves, peeled
5cm piece of fresh galangal (or use fresh root ginger), peeled
1 lemon grass stalk, trimmed and chopped
1 tbsp dried green peppercorns
1 tbsp unrefined dark muscovado sugar
1 tbsp fish sauce, plus extra if you like
2 tbsp freshly chopped coriander stalks
zest of 1 lime
1 tsp Thai shrimp paste

• •

To make the jungle curry paste, put the drained red chillies along with the rest of the curry paste ingredients into a food processor, then blitz to make a paste (or use a pestle and mortar to do this).

Heat the oil in a wok or heavy-based saucepan over a high heat, add the jungle curry paste and fry until the paste is fragrant (the chilli fragrance will scorch your throat!), stirring to prevent burning.

Add the turkey pieces and sauté for 2–3 minutes, then add the stock, aubergine, baby corn, snake beans and peas. Bring to the boil, then reduce the heat and simmer for around 5–7 minutes, or until the turkey is cooked, stirring occasionally.

Check the seasoning and add more fish sauce if you like. Garnish with the torn basil leaves and serve.

Hainanese Chicken

I truly love this recipe, as it's really simple and deliciously heart-warming. With a little preparation you can give yourself and your family a feast of a meal. Originally from China, this dish actually became popular in Singapore. Served with steamed brown rice and my home-made Sriracha hot sauce (see page 219), this will be a dish you'll find so easy to make and so pleasurable to eat that you'll prepare it again and again.

SERVES 6

PER SERVING:
CALORIES 270KCAL
FAT 15G
SUGAR 1G

2 tbsp light soy sauce
1 tbsp sake (rice wine)
4–5 black peppercorns
2 garlic cloves, roughly chopped
5cm piece of fresh root ginger (peel on), washed and sliced
3 spring onions, cut in half
1 x 1.5kg whole chicken, skin removed and fat trimmed
salt

Fill a large pan (big enough to comfortably hold the chicken) with water and add the soy sauce, sake and black peppercorns.

Place the garlic, ginger and spring onions into the cavity of the chicken and season with salt.

Add the chicken to the pot of seasoned water (leave the pot uncovered at this stage) and bring to a simmer over a low to medium heat, then cover with a lid and cook for 1 hour, or until the chicken is cooked and tender. Halfway through the cooking time, skim the surface to ensure a clear broth (I find the best way to do this is by using a tea strainer).

Remove from the heat. Transfer the chicken from the stock to a plate, cover with foil and leave to rest for around 15 minutes.

You can now reduce the stock by placing the pot (uncovered) back over a high heat for about 5 minutes. It should remain watery – similar to a thin, gravy-like sauce.

Carve the chicken and serve with the sauce poured over, some brown rice and sriracha.

Steamed Sea Bass Soup with Chinese Five-spice

Chinese five-spice powder is a great ingredient for livening up dishes, and a little goes a long way. Traditionally, it is made up of Sichuan peppercorns, star anise, cinnamon, cloves and fennel seeds, although I have come across some similar spice blends that also contain a variety of non-traditional spices like turmeric, nutmeg, ginger and sometimes mandarin peel. Chinese five-spice powder is readily available in many supermarkets.

SERVES 4

PER SERVING:
CALORIES 304KCAL
FAT 6G
SUGAR 6G

1 litre fish stock
1 tbsp fish sauce
3 garlic cloves, sliced
7.5cm piece of fresh root ginger, peeled and sliced
2 red chillies, cut in half lengthways
6 spring onions, sliced
1 tbsp light soy sauce

4 x 200g skinless and boneless sea bass fillets
1 tbsp Chinese five-spice powder
1 carrot, cut into thin strips
2 pak choi, each cut into 4 lenghtways
salt
extra chopped spring onions and some sesame oil, to garnish

To make the broth, put the fish stock in a saucepan with the fish sauce, garlic, ginger, chillies and half of the spring onions. Bring to the boil, add the soy sauce, then reduce the heat and keep the broth simmering.

Place the sea bass fillets in a greased bamboo or metal insert (that fits over the pan). Season with the five-spice powder and some salt, then place the carrot, pak choi and the remaining spring onions on top.

Place the bamboo insert over the simmering broth, cover and steam for 5–7 minutes until the fish is cooked.

Divide the steamed fish and vegetables into Chinese soup bowls and then ladle over the hot broth. Garnish each portion with extra chopped spring onions and a few drops of sesame oil and serve.

Sweet Chilli Chicken with Lemon

This is an addictive sweet-savoury recipe, with sourness from the lemon that lifts this dish to a different dimension. Virtually fat free, it is a healthy choice for feeding a crowd. I often cook this for an easy midweek supper when the girls swing by unexpectedly for a feeding!

SERVES 4

PER SERVING:
CALORIES 115KCAL
FAT 1G
SUGAR 4G

2 skinless and boneless chicken breast fillets
3 garlic cloves, grated
5cm piece of fresh root ginger, peeled and cut into thin matchsticks (julienned)
zest and juice of 1 lemon
2 tbsp sweet chilli sauce
1 pak choi, trimmed and cut in half lengthways
1 x 225g tin bamboo shoots, drained and rinsed
1 tbsp freshly chopped coriander

Slice the chicken breasts into thin strips and place in a non-metallic bowl. Add the garlic, ginger, lemon zest and juice and sweet chilli sauce and mix well. Cover and leave to marinate in the fridge for 1 hour.

Heat a wok over a high heat until hot, add the marinated chicken strips and cook until browned on the underside, around 3-4 minutes (don't stir as this allows the chicken to caramelise on the outside). Turn the chicken over and leave it to cook and caramelise on the other side for a few minutes. Add the pak choi and bamboo shoots and stir-fry for around 2 minutes.

Garnish with the coriander, then serve with rice vermicelli noodles and a mixed leaf salad.

Jambalaya

Probably one of the most famous Southern American Creole dishes, jambalaya was originally of Spanish and French influence, but it now has numerous variations across the Southern States of America and throughout the West Indies. I remember the first time I had this paella-type dish, I was around 9 years old and a friend's mum, who is from Trinidad, cooked me up her version. I loved it, and since then have created many different versions. This dish truly captures the beauty of one-pot cooking, it's so colourful and requires just one large pot to feed a family. Perfect.

SERVES 6

PER SERVING:
CALORIES 320KCAL
FAT 9G
SUGAR 6G

1 tbsp olive oil
1 Spanish onion, thinly sliced
500g pork tenderloin (trimmed of fat), cut into 2cm-thick slices
2 tbsp paprika
1 tbsp ground cumin
1 tsp ground allspice
50g chorizo, skinned and chopped into small cubes
3 garlic cloves, grated

1 red pepper, seeded and thinly sliced
1 yellow pepper, seeded and thinly sliced
100g French beans, cut at an angle into thirds
175g long-grain easy-cook brown rice
750ml chicken stock
salt

• •

Heat the oil in a large casserole over a medium heat and fry the onion for around 3–5 minutes until softened and starting to caramelise.

Season the pork slices with salt, then add them to the pan and sauté for 3 minutes until browned. Add the ground spices, chorizo, garlic, peppers and French beans and sauté for a further 2 minutes.

Add the rice and stir so all the grains are coated, then add the stock and bring to the boil. Once boiling, reduce the heat to a simmer, cover with a tight-fitting lid and simmer for 10 minutes, then uncover and simmer for a further 10 minutes.

Remove from the heat, re-cover and leave to rest with the lid firmly on for an additional 10 minutes.

When you remove the lid, the rice and meat will be perfectly cooked and tender and ready to serve.

Herby Pilaff

There are so many ways to cook pilaff, typically with rice and stock, but sometimes using toasted vermicelli with rice and stock to create a unique nutty-flavoured pilaff. This is really quick to put together and is a great way of cooking brown rice, packed full of fibre and fresh herbs. It works so well with fish, like my Butterflied Harissa Sardines (see page 55).

SERVES 4

PER SERVING:
CALORIES 385KCAL
FAT 12G
SUGAR 4G

1 tbsp olive oil
1 medium onion, finely chopped
2 garlic cloves, finely chopped
300g brown basmati rice
650ml vegetable stock
handful of coarsely
  chopped parsley
handful of finely snipped
  chives
handful of coarsely
  chopped coriander
3 tbsp toasted flaked almonds
salt and freshly ground
  black pepper

Heat the oil in a heavy-based sauté pan and cook the onion for 3–4 minutes until translucent. Add the garlic and seasoning and cook for 2 minutes.

Add the rice and stir to coat all the grains with oil, then pour over the stock. Bring to the boil, then reduce the heat, cover and simmer for 12-14 minutes.

Fork through the herbs and flaked almonds and serve.

Black Bean Chilli

I do love to have a few days a week where I eat only vegetarian food. I think there's a part of me that could quite possibly become vegetarian altogether. I'll let you know how I get on with that! I find that sometimes when I eat vegetarian food I need something that tastes 'meaty', is protein-rich and has depth of flavour. This black bean chilli definitely makes up for the lack of meat and is lower in fat and higher in fibre too. It's actually even better when made the day before and left to let the flavours permeate overnight in the fridge, before it is then reheated thoroughly the next day.

SERVES 8

PER SERVING:
CALORIES 100KCAL
FAT 2G
SUGAR 5G

2 x 400g tins black beans, drained and rinsed
1 x 400g tin peeled plum tomatoes, plus 2 tinfuls of cold water
1 Spanish onion, coarsely chopped
6 garlic cloves, finely chopped
1 tbsp olive oil
1 tbsp unrefined light muscovado sugar
10 sprigs of thyme

2 tsp ground cumin
1 tsp ground coriander
1 black cardamom pod (left whole)
1 tsp cayenne
1 tsp fennel seeds
salt and freshly ground black pepper
1 fennel bulb, shaved, and crumbled feta, to garnish

• • • • · · · • • • — · · · — • • • · · · · • • • — — · · · • • • • · · · • • • — · · · — • • • · · · • • • • · · · ·

Place all the ingredients (except the garnish) into a large, heavy-based pan and add salt and pepper to taste. Bring to the boil, then reduce the heat, cover and simmer for 1½ hours, stirring occasionally.

To garnish, top with shaved fennel and feta crumbled over, and serve.

Seafood Gumbo

A Louisiana staple, gumbo dates back to the 18th century and has a strong and powerful flavour. It is traditionally made using okra, also known as lady's fingers, and served with rice. Most Creole and Cajun dishes start off with a heavily seasoned roux sauce (béchamel white sauce), but I find that this makes the dish quite heavy and also requires a lot of fat for the desired effect. This feast of prawns, crabs and mussels is a much lighter version, with the addition of cornflour instead of a roux. All the flavours work really well when cooked together; the Creole spice with the okra and seafood is so satisfying, and the dish is great as an occasional treat. I like to serve it alongside steamed vegetables and salad, and a healthy dash of Tabasco sauce!

SERVES 6

PER SERVING:
CALORIES 210KCAL
FAT 6G
SUGAR 5G

1 tbsp vegetable oil
1 onion, finely chopped
1 carrot, finely chopped
1 green pepper, seeded and finely chopped
1 stick celery, finely chopped
1 bay leaf
1 tbsp cornflour
1 litre chicken stock, at room temperature
1 tbsp cayenne

200g fresh okra, chopped at an angle
300g raw king prawns, heads and shells left on
1kg freshly cooked crabs (any kind), cut into pieces, shell on (ask your fishmonger to prepare this for you)
300g fresh live mussels, cleaned (see Note below)
2 tbsp freshly chopped parsley
Tabasco sauce, to taste

• •

Heat the oil in a large casserole over a medium heat, add the onion, carrot, green pepper, celery and bay leaf and sauté for 10 minutes until the vegetables have softened and are starting to caramelise.

Meanwhile, put the cornflour into a small jug, add around 3 tablespoons of cold water and whisk together until completely smooth.

Add the stock and cayenne to the casserole along with the cornflour mixture, then cook for a few minutes, stirring, until the stock starts to bubble on the surface. Add the okra and seafood, then cover and cook for 10 minutes. The mussels are cooked when their shells have opened – discard any mussels that remain firmly closed.

Remove from the heat, then sprinkle the gumbo with the parsley and season to taste with Tabasco sauce. Serve.

NOTE
Clean the mussels well in cold water and remove the beards. Discard any mussels with broken shells or any that do not close when firmly tapped with the back of a knife.

Beef Rendang

This dish originates from Indonesia. It is made by simmering beef for several hours in coconut milk and spices, until the liquid has evaporated and you're left with a really intense and thick sauce that coats the pieces of meat. I prefer a bit more sauce for my rendang, so I don't cook it down for so long that all the sauce has evaporated. I like to serve it with the Lime and Mustard Rice with Curry Leaves (see page 101).

SERVES 6

PER SERVING:
CALORIES 220KCAL
FAT 10G
SUGAR 6G

10 large dried red chillies, soaked in hot water and drained (see page 17)
4 banana shallots, halved
4 garlic cloves, peeled
7.5cm piece of fresh root ginger, peeled
7.5cm piece of fresh galangal, peeled
2.5cm piece of fresh turmeric, peeled
1 x 400ml tin light coconut milk
1 tbsp unrefined dark muscovado sugar
600g lean braising beef, trimmed of fat and cut into 7.5cm cubes

6 kaffir lime leaves
2 lemon grass stalks, trimmed, bruised and bent in half
800ml vegetable stock
3 tbsp freshly chopped coriander

FOR THE SPICE BLEND
2 tsp fennel seeds
2 tsp coriander seeds
1 tsp cumin seeds
1 tsp black peppercorns
1 tsp ground cinnamon
1 green cardamom pod, left whole but smashed open

• •

To make the spice blend, using a clean coffee grinder, grind all the spices together to a powder (this could also be done using a pestle and mortar).

Put the spice blend powder into a food processor. Add the drained red chillies along with the shallots, garlic, ginger, galangal and turmeric, then blitz to a smooth paste.

Put 4 tablespoons of the coconut milk into a heavy-based casserole over a medium heat and leave it to bubble for a few minutes. Add the rendang paste and leave it to bubble and cook for 5 minutes. When the coconut milk starts to split (you'll see oil beginning to come to the surface), stir in the sugar.

Add the beef, lime leaves and lemon grass, then leave the beef to brown, turning occasionally. If it becomes too dry, you can add another tablespoon or so of coconut milk.

Once the beef is browned, in around 5 minutes, add the rest of the coconut milk and the stock. Bring to a gentle boil, then cover and cook over a medium to low heat for 2 hours, stirring occasionally. Once cooked, the beef should be so tender that it falls apart when prodded.

Shred the beef into the sauce and then stir through the coriander. Serve with plain brown rice or Lime and Mustard Rice with Curry Leaves.

Classic Chinese Congee

I have to say, the first time I tried congee (a type of savoury porridge) I was not impressed; it was congealed and gloopy, and was served as part of a breakfast buffet. I found I couldn't stomach it first thing in the morning. I realise now that my first reaction to this dish was due to bad cooking. I tried it again a couple of years ago and was really surprised at how much I liked it. I really enjoy this dish on a cold winter's night after a long stressful day at work. It's easy to prepare and easy to eat, and ticks all the comfort food boxes. If you have any leftover roast meat, you can add it to the congee for extra flavour.

SERVES 6

PER SERVING:
CALORIES 110KCAL
FAT 1G
SUGAR 3G

10 dried shiitake mushrooms
100g long-grain white rice
1.5 litres vegetable stock
4 garlic cloves, smashed
7.5cm piece of fresh root ginger (peel on), washed and sliced into discs
2 spring onions, cut in half
2 tbsp light soy sauce
salt

TO SERVE AND GARNISH
leftover cold roast chicken, torn into pieces
fresh root ginger, peeled and cut into matchsticks (julienned)
finely sliced spring onions
Sriracha (see page 219)
light soy sauce

Put the shiitake mushrooms into a heatproof bowl, pour over enough hot water to cover and leave to soak for 2 hours. Drain (reserving the soaking water to add to the congee), then slice the mushrooms.

Put the rice into a sieve, then rinse and drain it 3 times under cold running water to remove some of the starch.

Put the rice, stock, garlic, ginger discs, halved spring onions, shiitake mushrooms and reserved soaking water into a large casserole. Bring to the boil, then reduce the heat, cover and simmer for around 1¼ hours, stirring every 10–15 minutes so that the rice doesn't stick to the casserole. (Note – the longer you cook this mixture, the denser it becomes, so if you want a lighter congee 1 hour cooking time will be sufficient.)

Stir in the soy sauce, then remove from the heat. Season to taste with salt.

To serve, lay out the roast chicken, the ginger and spring onion garnishes, the sriracha and soy sauce alongside the congee, and encourage everyone to serve themselves.

Chana Dahl and Curry Leaves

Dahl is an Indian lentil soup that I find to be one of the most satisfying dishes to eat, and I'm sure you will too once you've perfected the spices and found the thickness that you enjoy best. This is my go-to staple, particularly when I need something to lift my spirits. It's is a dish that makes me think I could go vegetarian, as it is so heart-warming and filling that it makes me desire nothing else. It's rich in carbohydrates for energy thanks to the lentils, which also have a low glycemic index rating so are great for keeping hunger at bay without giving you a blood-sugar spike. They are also rich in fibre, B vitamins and zinc (a good immunity booster), so an all-round healthy choice! Once you've got used to cooking this, you can play around with spices that you like and make it thinner or thicker depending on taste.

SERVES 4

PER SERVING:
CALORIES 324KCAL
FAT 16G
SUGAR 2G

200g dried chana dahl (yellow spit peas)
6 green chillies, split in half lengthways
¼ brown coconut, flesh grated (or you could use 100g desiccated coconut instead)

2 tsp ground cumin
1 tsp hot chilli powder
1 tsp ground coriander
1 tsp garam masala
1 tsp ground turmeric
12 fresh curry leaves

Place the chana dahl in a heavy-based saucepan with 1 litre cold water and bring to the boil. Remove the scum and foam that rises to the surface – the best way to skim this off is using a large metal spoon.

Add all the other ingredients to the pan, then cover and cook for 30–40 minutes until the dahl has softened and takes on a thick soup-like consistency. Stir occasionally and add a little more water if you think the mixture is becoming too dry.

Serve as part of a meal with rice and salad. To finish, I like to top this off with a spoonful of my Coconut Chutney (see page 215).

West Indian Pepper Pot

One of the Caribbean's infamously spicy dishes, pepper pot is traditionally made in a Dutch pot. It is full of heat from the scotch bonnet with a more mellow touch of spices such as allspice and cinnamon. You can use whichever vegetables you like for a pepper pot but the spices and seasoning should have a good balance. When you cook using a Dutch pot, the pot gradually becomes 'seasoned' in a similar way to a wok, and somehow whenever you cook with it, it adds that extra *je ne sais quoi.* If you don't have a seasoned Dutch pot, a heavy casserole is perfectly fine to use instead, but, if you ever wonder why your pepper pot doesn't taste quite like the stuff you get in hard food joints, you'll know the reason why! Packed with antioxidant nutrients, this makes a healthy, satisfying midweek meal.

SERVES 3

PER SERVING:
CALORIES 330KCAL
FAT 11G
SUGAR 16G

2 tbsp vegetable oil
1 large Spanish onion, finely diced
10 sprigs of thyme
1 tsp dried marjoram
1 tsp ground allspice
1 tsp ground cinnamon
1 tsp ground cloves
½ tsp ground nutmeg
1 scotch bonnet chilli, finely diced
1 red pepper, seeded and cut into cubes

1 large sweet potato, peeled and cut into 5cm cubes
20 fresh okra, cut into 2cm pieces
300g kale with stems, roughly chopped
600ml vegetable stock
200g fresh spinach with stems, roughly chopped
salt
freshly snipped chives and finely chopped spring onions, to finish

Heat the oil in a Dutch pot or heavy-based casserole over a medium heat, add the onion, thyme sprigs and dried marjoram and cook for 5 minutes until the onion softens. Add the ground spices and scotch bonnet and sauté for 1 minute until fragrant.

Add all the remaining ingredients (except the spinach, chives and spring onions) and season with salt. Bring to the boil, then reduce the heat, cover and simmer for 30 minutes, stirring occasionally.

Stir in the spinach, re-cover the pan and cook for a further 10 minutes.

Stir in the chives and spring onions, and serve.

African Pepper Soup

The first time I came across this dish was at university when I was feeling a bit low and tired from all the late-night studying. I was missing home and I needed a meal that was going to make me feel better (and it needed to be something I could eat while tucked up in bed feeling sorry for myself). Chicken soup is a tried and tested 'remedy' across the world that is meant to make you feel better with its soothing and healing qualities. Well, think of how standard chicken soup makes you feel, then add a handful of African ingredients and love and you'll understand how this soup was my dish of salvation. Every time I cook this I always have a huge smile on my face, remembering my university girls and the good times we all had together.

SERVES 4

PER SERVING:
CALORIES 365KCAL
FAT 10G
SUGAR 15G

600g skinless chicken legs
1 onion, thinly sliced
2 garlic cloves, smashed
1 scotch bonnet chilli, left whole
2 plantain, peeled and cut into 7.5cm pieces
1 small yam, peeled and cut into 7.5cm pieces
30g dried crayfish (if you can't get this, you can use 2 tbsp shrimp paste instead)
2 chicken stock cubes, crumbled
1 tsp hot chilli powder
1 tsp ground ginger

· ·

I find that the easiest way to make this soup is to put all the ingredients into one big pan and add 1.5 litres of cold water.

Bring to the boil, then cover and cook over a low to medium heat for 1½ hours until the chicken is cooked and really tender. Serve immediately.

Beef and Plantain Mexican Mole

Mole is a classic Mexican dish that can be quite confusing the first time you eat it. If you didn't know, you'd never guess there was chocolate in the dish, and when you do know, you half expect it to taste sweet, but it's a savoury, dark, rich and subtly spiced stew. The chocolate (in the form of cocoa powder here) actually enhances the savouriness of the dish and really is quite a taste sensation.

SERVES 6

PER SERVING:
CALORIES 342KCAL
FAT 14G
SUGAR 11G

1 tbsp vegetable oil
500g lean braising beef (trimmed of fat), cut into 5cm cubes
2 plantain, peeled and cut into 1cm rounds
1 litre vegetable stock
salt
lime wedges, to serve

FOR THE PASTE
30g sesame seeds
30g pumpkin seeds
2 red or green jalapeño chillies
2 tsp ground cinnamon
1 tsp ground allspice
1 tbsp dried thyme
1 tsp dried oregano
75g good-quality unsweetened dark/bitter cocoa powder
1 onion, chopped
3 garlic cloves, peeled

First make the paste. In a small hand blender/chopper, blitz together the sesame seeds, pumpkin seeds, jalapeño chillies, ground spices, dried herbs, cocoa powder, onion and garlic until you get a smooth paste. Set aside.

Heat the oil in a large, heavy-based pan over a medium heat, add the beef and cook until browned all over, around 5–7 minutes.

Stir in the paste and leave to bubble and become fragrant, around a few minutes. Add the plantain and stock and season with salt. Bring to the boil, then reduce the heat, cover with a lid and simmer for 1½ hours, stirring from time to time.

Serve with lime wedges to squeeze the juice over.

Lime and Mustard Rice with Curry Leaves

This is a perfect accompaniment to many dishes in this book. I guarantee that, after you've made it once, you'll keep making it again and again! The most important thing is to ensure that the rice is hot when you add it to the spice mix, as it all needs to come together at the same time so that all the flavours meld and combine perfectly.

SERVES 4

PER SERVING:
CALORIES 214KCAL
FAT 4G
SUGAR NONE

200g basmati rice
1 tbsp mustard oil
5 kaffir lime leaves
2 tbsp black mustard seeds
handful of fresh curry leaves
zest and juice of 1 lime
handful of roughly
    chopped coriander
salt and freshly ground
    black pepper

Bring a large pan of lightly salted water to the boil, add the basmati rice and cook for 10 minutes. Drain, set aside and keep hot.

Wipe the rice-cooking pan dry with a tea towel, then place it over a medium heat. Add the mustard oil, followed by the lime leaves, mustard seeds and curry leaves and cook for 1 minute. Season with salt and pepper, then add the lime zest and juice and the hot rice. Reduce to a low simmer, cover with a tight-fitting lid and cook for 2–3 minutes.

Remove from the heat and leave the rice to sit with the lid still firmly on for 5 minutes. Uncover and carefully fork through the coriander. Serve.

Korean Brown Rice and Brussels Sprouts

This is a delicious Korean fried rice dish made using cooked brown rice and Brussels Sprout Kimchi (see page 218). It is a great way of using up leftovers, and you can add whichever vegetables and meat you have in your fridge. I think every culture that eats a lot of rice will always have many ways of using up leftover cooked rice.

A quick tip for cooking the perfect brown rice is to rinse the grains thoroughly in cold running water before cooking to remove some of the starch, then cook the rice just slightly less than the timings given on the packet, so that it retains its nutty bite.

SERVES 4

PER SERVING:
CALORIES 184KCAL
FAT 7G
SUGAR 5G

2 tbsp vegetable oil
1 garlic clove, finely chopped
1 medium leek, washed and finely chopped
¼ Savoy cabbage, finely chopped
125g Brussels Sprout Kimchi (see page 218)

250g leftover cold cooked brown basmati rice
2 spring onions, finely chopped
1 tbsp light soy sauce
1 tbsp oyster sauce

• • • ·· • • • · ·· ·· • • · · • · ·· · ·· • • • · · • · ·· • • • · • • • • · ·· • • • ·· · ·

Heat the oil in a wok over a high heat and stir-fry the garlic, leek and cabbage for a few minutes until they start to soften.

Add the kimchi and cooked rice and stir-fry for 3 minutes. Add the spring onions, soy sauce and oyster sauce and stir-fry for a final 1 minute. Serve.

Sardines with Ras el Hanout and Fennel

Ras el hanout is a beautiful combination of around 25–30 spices from Morocco, and its name translates as 'top of the shop' or 'head of the shop' – basically meaning that the shopkeepers make their own unique blend, which may include flavourings ranging from cumin and coriander seeds to orange peel and rose petals. It's so unique in flavour and can lift up any dish. It works really well with sardines because these strong oily fish can take a lot of punchy spice, and the fennel here is the perfect partner to balance the oiliness and spiciness of the dish. I absolutely love this dish and I hope you do too!

SERVES 4

PER SERVING:
CALORIES 425KCAL
FAT 25G
SUGAR 4G

8 fresh sardines, gutted, scaled and cleaned
2 tbsp ras el hanout spice mix
2 tbsp olive oil
2 small fennel bulbs, quartered
2 large plum tomatoes, quartered
1 lemon, cut into wedges
freshly chopped parsley, to garnish

• •

Dust the sardines all over with the ras el hanout.

Heat the oil in a large (lidded) skillet pan over a medium heat. Carefully lay the spice-dusted sardines in a single layer in the pan, leaving a little space between each one.

Carefully nestle the fennel and tomato quarters and the lemon wedges around the fish, cover the skillet with a lid and leave to cook for 10 minutes.

Remove from the heat, keep the lid on and leave to rest for a few minutes before serving.

Squeeze over some of the warm lemon juice from the wedges, garnish with chopped parsley and serve. This is perfect with Beetroot and Orange with Pimento (see page 71).

Malay Laksa Lemak

This fragrant coconut and noodle soup is creamy and spicy and is a complete meal in itself. In this recipe I like to use fish balls, which you can get from Chinese supermarkets, but if you are not fond of the texture you could replace them with some firm set (original) tofu, which you can dice and place straight into the dish. The most important thing is to make sure you get the paste right. Once you've mastered that then the whole dish will come together. The great thing about this dish is that it's all according to taste, so you can add as much or as little of the spices as you like.

SERVES 4

PER SERVING:
CALORIES 516KCAL
FAT 11G
SUGAR 3G

1 tbsp vegetable oil
1 x 400ml tin light coconut milk
800ml fish stock
leaves from 2 sprigs of Vietnamese mint, plus extra to garnish
200g mixed baby corn and mangetout
12 fish balls
2 small fresh squid, cleaned and cut into 5mm-thick rings
10 fresh live black mussels, scrubbed clean and de-bearded (see Note on page 90)
300g dried rice vermicelli noodles

FOR THE SPICE PASTE
2 lemon grass stalks, trimmed
2 garlic cloves, peeled
3cm piece of fresh turmeric, peeled
3cm piece of fresh root ginger, peeled
1 tbsp coriander seeds
1 tbsp shrimp paste
2 red chillies

• •

To make the spice paste, place all the ingredients in a food processor, add a few tablespoons of cold water and blitz to make a coarse paste.

Heat the oil in a heavy-based saucepan, add the spice paste and cook for a few minutes until fragrant, stirring constantly so the paste doesn't burn. Add the coconut milk, stock and mint leaves, bring to the boil, then reduce the heat and simmer, uncovered, for 10 minutes.

Add the mixed vegetables, fish balls and seafood, then cover and cook for 5 minutes. By this stage, the fish balls and seafood will be cooked through – discard any cooked mussels that remain firmly closed.

Meanwhile, place the noodles in a large, heatproof bowl, cover with boiling water and leave to soak for around 5 minutes (or according to packet instructions) until tender, then drain.

Stir the noodles into the seafood mixture, garnish with extra mint and serve.

Sri Lankan Butternut Squash Curry

One evening my sister's friend and her mum showed me how to cook some traditional Sri Lankan dishes, and this was one of the stand-out dishes of the night. I was most impressed that it didn't require the spices to be tempered or even roasted, yet the end result was a heady, layered and aromatic vegetable curry. This recipe's simplicity is what makes it so special. The curry is perfect as a midweek get-together meal, particularly if you've come home after work wanting something really easy but delicious to prepare. (See photographs overleaf.)

SERVES 6

PER SERVING:
CALORIES 215KCAL
FAT 9G
SUGAR 13G

1 large butternut squash, seeded (skin left on) and cut into 5cm cubes
1 onion, chopped into large chunks
3 tbsp desiccated coconut
1 x 400ml tin light coconut milk, plus 1 tinful of cold water
2 tbsp ground coriander
1 tsp white pepper
1 tsp ground turmeric
1 tsp fenugreek seeds
1 tsp hot chilli powder
2 green cardamom pods, left whole but lightly crushed
1 cinnamon stick, snapped in half
6 fresh curry leaves, plus extra to garnish
salt

• •

Put all the ingredients into a heavy-based casserole or saucepan and season with salt to taste. Bring to a gentle boil, then cook, uncovered, over a medium heat for around 45 minutes, or until the squash is cooked and tender, stirring occasionally.

Garnish with extra curry leaves and serve with brown rice and salad.

FINGER FOOD & SHARING PLATES

'Eat everything in moderation, choose ingredients that are delicious but won't impact negatively on your health.'

FINGER FOOD & SHARING PLATES

I love having friends and family over and having a range of dishes made ahead for everyone to enjoy. The recipes in this chapter are ideal for entertaining, and are really delicious and good for you too.

Don't just save them for parties though, get these recipes out whenever you have guests around and fancy a relaxed evening meal. Or choose a selection of recipes and serve with a large green salad for an informal lunch.

Often party food and nibbles can be high in fat and it's all too easy to overindulge. What I tend to do now is make lots of tasty nibbles that are lighter and use lower-in-fat ingredients but still pack a flavour punch.

This chapter is dedicated to people who, just like me, enjoy hosting parties with delicious nibbles but are looking for alternative, inspiring and healthier options.

Spring Roll Party

Vietnamese spring rolls can come in a variety of flavours, and unlike the deep-fried Chinese-style spring rolls, these are fresh, uncooked rolls made using soaked rice paper wrappers filled with fresh vegetables, cooked rice vermicelli noodles and a choice of either cooked pork or prawns (see photographs pages 116–117).

You can serve these alongside dipping sauces; for the incredibly brave, you can try Nam Pla Prik (see page 217) or my lovely Sriracha (see page 219). In my opinion, the more condiments the better here, so have ready a variety of your favourite dipping sauces.

**MAKES 16
SPRING ROLLS**

PER ROLL:
CALORIES 85KCAL
FAT NONE
SUGAR 2G

100g dried rice vermicelli
  noodles
16 rice paper wrappers
  (see Notes opposite)
32 cooked, peeled king prawns,
  halved lengthways
3 spring onions, cut into
  matchsticks (julienned)
1 bunch each of mint, basil
  and coriander, leaves freshly
  chopped or torn

3 large red chillies, seeded
  and sliced into rings
1 medium cucumber, cut into
  matchsticks (julienned)
  (see Notes opposite)
2 medium carrots, peeled and cut
  into matchsticks (julienned)
  (see Notes opposite)
16 Little Gem lettuce leaves

• •

Place the noodles in a heatproof bowl, cover with boiling water and leave to soak for around 5 minutes (or according to packet instructions) until tender, then drain and leave to cool.

Place a clean, damp tea towel on a work surface. Fill a medium-sized shallow dish – big enough to hold a rice paper wrapper – with warm water.

Make 1 spring roll at a time. Place 1 rice paper wrapper in the warm water and leave until it becomes soft enough to roll, about 15 seconds. You don't want it to get too soft otherwise it will tear. (Getting this right will take a bit of trial and error, but you'll be fine once you get into the swing of it and find your way – it took me many attempts on my first go!)

Remove the wrapper from the water and place it on the damp tea towel. Lay 4 prawn halves (2 whole prawns per roll) along the centre of the wrapper, and then top with some spring onions, herbs, chillies, cucumber, carrots and rice vermicelli noodles, plus a lettuce leaf.

Bring the sides of the wrapper together, then tightly roll the wrapper around the filling to enclose it completely in the shape of a cigar (the same process you use to roll a closed tortilla or burrito).

Turn the roll over so the prawn layer faces upwards and then place it on a baking sheet lined with clingfilm. Cover with clingfilm. Carry on making the rest of the rolls in the same way until all the wrappers and filling ingredients are used up. Serve immediately.

NOTES

I use standard size rice paper wrappers here, which are readily available in specialist Asian supermarkets or international food stores.

You can replace the cucumber and carrots with any vegetables of your choice – this is just for guidance.

Mexican Bean Dip

This low-in-fat, high-in-fibre and protein dip requires no cooking and is easy to prepare, so it's perfect if you have unexpected guests popping over with little or no notice. You can whizz it up in no time and serve it with either vegetable crudités or whatever you have hanging about in your fridge, some baked tortilla wraps broken into shards or some toasted wholemeal pitta bread.

**SERVES 4
(AS PART OF A MEZE)**

PER SERVING:
CALORIES 76KCAL
FAT 1G
SUGAR 2G

1 x 400g tin red kidney beans, drained and rinsed
1 garlic clove, peeled
1 tsp paprika
1 tsp ground allspice
juice of 1 lime
salt and freshly ground black pepper

. . . .

Put all the ingredients into a food processor and blitz until completely smooth. Adjust the seasoning to taste. Serve immediately.

NOTE
You can also freeze this dip, if you like. I suggest making a bigger batch, then you can freeze it in an airtight container for up to 1 month. Defrost thoroughly in the fridge before serving.

Turkey Shawarma

Shawarma has a bad reputation among some people for being unhealthy and fatty, but typically this would be because of the side dishes or the way it is served – and people's late-night, beer-fuelled attempts at sobriety when ordering it may be another reason! Shawarma can be made from chicken, turkey, lamb or even beef, and typically it is cooked on a spit that rotates very slowly, enabling the meat to become really succulent and full of flavour. Using turkey breast instead of lamb or beef results in a lower fat content. Usually shawarma is served with a range of pickles, and perhaps some fattoush (a Middle Eastern salad) or even some tabbouleh. You could serve this alongside the Kale and Sumac Tabbouleh (see page 66) for a complete meal, but here it works well as individual portions for a party. You'll need to start this a few hours ahead or the day before you want to serve it, to give the turkey time to marinate.

SERVES 8
(AS PART OF A MEZE)

PER SERVING:
CALORIES 184KCAL
FAT 6G
SUGAR 1G

3 tbsp olive oil
1 tbsp ground cumin
1 tbsp ground coriander
1 tbsp paprika
zest of 1 lemon
1 garlic clove, grated
2.5cm piece of fresh root
    ginger, peeled and grated

4 turkey breast steaks
    (about 400g total weight)
50g low-fat natural yoghurt
1 tbsp Harissa (see page 212)
4 wholemeal pitta breads
large handful of roughly
    chopped mint leaves,
    to garnish

• •

Put the oil, ground spices, lemon zest, garlic and ginger into a large, shallow bowl or dish and mix together to form a marinade, then add the turkey breast steaks, turning to coat all over. Cover with clingfilm and leave to marinate in the fridge for at least 3 hours or overnight.

Heat a heavy-based frying pan over a medium heat until hot, add the marinated turkey steaks and cook for around 4–5 minutes on each side, or until the turkey is thoroughly cooked and has no pink meat and the juices run clear. Remove from the heat, leave to cool slightly, then carve into long strips.

Meanwhile, combine the yoghurt and harissa in a small bowl. Toast the pitta breads, cut them in half and then split open.

Serve the warm turkey strips in the toasted pitta halves, drizzle over some harissa yoghurt and sprinkle with chopped mint to garnish.

Chickpea Burgers with Tzatziki

Tzatziki yoghurt sauce always transports me to the Mediterranean region, where meze excites me and grabs my attention. The first time I ever sampled a proper tzatziki was about 8 years ago in Cyprus, where it was served alongside some grilled kid souvlaki – the sharp tang of garlic and refreshing mix of herbs tempered the heavy and rich kid meat. Typically, the flavour of tzatziki is sharp, herby, garlicky and lemony – the degree of intensity of these flavours is entirely down to personal preference.

MAKES 8 BURGERS

PER BURGER:
CALORIES 140KCAL
FAT 3G
SUGAR 1G

FOR THE BURGERS
1 x 410g tin chickpeas, drained and rinsed
1 red chilli
2 tsp mild curry powder
handful each of freshly chopped parsley and coriander
2 eggs
150g breadcrumbs (fresh or dried)

FOR THE TZATZIKI
¼ cucumber, grated
handful of freshly chopped mint leaves
100g 0%-fat Greek-style yoghurt
½ garlic clove, grated
juice of ½ lemon
salt

To make the burgers, place the chickpeas, chilli, curry powder, herbs, eggs and breadcrumbs in a food processor. Pulse together to make a thick, firm paste. Using wet hands, shape the mixture into 8 patties.

Heat a frying pan over a medium heat until hot, then cook the patties for 3–4 minutes on each side until browned.

Meanwhile, to make the tzatziki, place all the ingredients in a bowl and mix together. Adjust the salt to taste.

Arrange the chickpea burgers on a platter, serve the tzatziki alongside and encourage everyone to share.

Chicken and Asparagus Yakitori

Yakitori is the perfect Japanese snack to serve at a party, usually accompanied by beer or shochu (a distilled alcohol). Mirin, soy sauce, sake (rice wine) and sugar are the main ingredients that make up a simple yakitori glaze, and this recipe is easy to make and light to eat. You can prepare a bigger batch of glaze, then keep it in an airtight container in the fridge for up to 3 days to use in a stir-fry or to marinate meat or fish. Its versatile flavour creates a perfect everyday sauce or marinade.

MAKES 12 SKEWERS

PER SKEWER:
CALORIES 38KCAL
FAT NONE
SUGAR 2G

250g skinless and boneless chicken breast fillets (trimmed of fat), cut into 2.5cm pieces
10 fresh asparagus spears, cut into 5cm pieces

FOR THE GLAZE
2 tbsp mirin
2 tbsp light soy sauce
2 tbsp sake (rice wine)
1 tsp unrefined light muscovado sugar

• • • ·· • • • • ·· • • • ·· • • • ·· • • • ·· • • • ·· • • • ·· • • • ·· • • • ·· • • • ·· • ·· • •

Thread the chicken and asparagus onto 12 pre-soaked wooden skewers, alternating the two ingredients.

In a small bowl, mix together the glaze ingredients.

Heat a griddle pan over a high heat until searing hot, add the chicken and asparagus skewers and brush with the glaze. Keep turning and brushing the skewers with the glaze until the chicken and asparagus are cooked and slightly charred all over, around 5 minutes. Serve.

Thai Chicken Satay

A classic party nibble, which is a favourite for everyone. This is a fuss-free and simple way of making a party staple, which you will go back to again and again.

MAKES 16 SKEWERS

PER SKEWER:
CALORIES 95KCAL
FAT 4G
SUGAR 3G

4 skinless and boneless
    chicken breast fillets

FOR THE MARINADE
3 garlic cloves, grated
5cm piece of fresh root
    ginger, peeled and grated
4 tbsp dark soy sauce
juice of 1 lime
1 tbsp ground coriander
1 tsp ground turmeric

**FOR THE PEANUT
DIPPING SAUCE**
100g unsalted roasted peanuts
150ml light coconut milk
2 garlic cloves, peeled
2.5cm piece of fresh root
    ginger, peeled
juice of 1 lime
2 tbsp unrefined light
    muscovado sugar
2 tbsp dark soy sauce

• •

Soak 12–16 wooden skewers in water for 15 minutes before use, then drain.

Slice the chicken fillets lengthways into thin strips. Combine all the marinade ingredients in a mixing bowl, then add the chicken and toss well to coat all over, rubbing the marinade into the meat. Thread the chicken onto the soaked skewers, about 2 or so strips per skewer. Place the skewers on a baking tray, cover with clingfilm and chill in the fridge for at least 1 hour or overnight.

On the day that you are serving the satay, make the peanut dipping sauce. Place all the ingredients in a food processor along with 200ml cold water. Blitz to form a nice smooth sauce. Transfer to a bowl and keep in the fridge until you are ready to serve.

Remove the chicken from the fridge about 10 minutes before cooking.

Meanwhile, preheat the oven to 180°C/gas 4.

Cook the tray of chicken skewers in the preheated oven for around 15 minutes until thoroughly cooked. Serve with the peanut dipping sauce on the side.

Ayam Goreng CHICKEN WINGS WITH TAMARIND SAMBAL

Sambals are types of chilli-based sauces that are made across South-east Asia, and a range can be found in specialist Asian supermarkets and international food stores around the country. The most common tends to be sambal oelek, named after how it is made using a pestle and mortar. The ingredients in sambals can vary, but typically a sambal adds a fiery, deep umami flavour that is enriched with either anchovies, dried shrimp or fish sauce/paste. Here, the tamarind sambal makes these chicken wings so deliciously moreish (see photographs pages 124–125).

SERVES 8

PER SERVING:
CALORIES 231KCAL
FAT 13G
SUGAR 9G

1kg chicken wings (skin left on)

FOR THE MARINADE
4 tbsp dark soy sauce
2 tbsp fish sauce
2 tbsp fresh lemon juice
3 garlic cloves, finely chopped
2–3 red bird's eye chillies, finely chopped

FOR THE TAMARIND SAMBAL
5 dried red chillies, soaked in hot water and drained (see page 17)

5 garlic cloves, peeled
1 banana shallot, cut in half
2 tbsp palm sugar
2 tbsp tamarind paste
1 tbsp fish sauce
1 tsp shrimp paste
2 tbsp vegetable oil
freshly torn mixed herbs, such as mint, basil and coriander leaves, to garnish
lime wedges, to serve

• •

Put the chicken wings in a large bowl. In a separate small bowl, combine all the marinade ingredients, then pour this over the chicken and toss to coat all over. Cover and leave to marinate in the fridge for 1 hour.

Meanwhile, make the sambal: put the drained chillies and all the remaining ingredients (except the oil, herbs and lime wedges) into a food processor and blitz until smooth. Heat the oil in a saucepan over a medium to high heat, tip in the sambal and cook for a few minutes until fragrant, stirring occasionally. Remove from the heat and leave to cool to room temperature.

In the meantime, take the marinated chicken wings out of the fridge and leave to come up to room temperature. Preheat the oven to 200°C/gas 6.

Place the chicken wings in a single layer on a baking tray. Cook in the preheated oven for 30 minutes, or until golden and crispy.

Transfer the cooked wings to a serving bowl, then toss through the sambal so that each wing is coated. Garnish with the torn herbs and serve with wedges of lime.

Aubergine Dip with Pomegranate and Pine Nuts

There are variants across the Middle East for the aubergine dish *baba ghannouj* (better known here as baba ghanoush) and there are disputes far and wide as to its origins. This recipe is inspired by baba ghannoush, but the method is easier and there is a more complex flavour profile here with the addition of pine nuts and pomegranate. Typically in baba ghannoush, aubergines are rotated over a flame and the skin is blackened as they cook. Once all the skin is charred the aubergines are left to cool and then the flesh, which has turned creamy, is scraped out to create the baba ghannoush. The method here is easier as you don't have to watch or stand over the aubergine during cooking, you just place it in the oven and let it do its thing.

**SERVES 6
(AS PART OF A MEZE)**

PER SERVING:
CALORIES 54KCAL
FAT 1G
SUGAR 5G

2 aubergines, cut in half lengthways
1 tsp cumin seeds
1 tsp coriander seeds, ground
1 tsp smoked paprika
4 garlic cloves, finely chopped
2 shallots, chopped
1 tsp fresh lemon juice
seeds of ½ pomegranate (remove any bitter white pith), plus a few extra seeds to garnish

handful of freshly chopped parsley
10 mint leaves, chopped
salt and freshly ground black pepper
2 tbsp toasted pine nuts, to garnish

Preheat the oven to 180°C/gas 4.

Put the aubergine halves, cut sides uppermost, in a shallow ovenproof dish or roasting tin, then sprinkle over the spices, garlic and shallots. Cook in the preheated oven for 30 minutes until charred and the flesh is soft.

Remove from the oven, leave to cool completely (the aubergines are easier to handle when cooled), then scrape away the flesh into a bowl and discard the skin. Add the lemon juice, pomegranate seeds, parsley and mint and mix well. Season to taste with salt and pepper.

Garnish with the toasted pine nuts and a few more pomegranate seeds sprinkled over. Serve the dip with toasted pitta and vegetable crudités, or simply on its own with grilled lean meat.

Baked Haloumi with Garlic and Mint Dressing

Traditional nomadic Bedouin life in the Middle East required moving from one place to another, usually through harsh weather conditions and intense heat. Bedouin communities needed food that would travel well and not spoil, therefore historically haloumi cheese has been an ideal travel companion as it has a long shelf life and high tolerance of heat. Usually made with goat's milk and stored in brine, haloumi is ideal for grilling, frying and baking as it holds its texture and shape really well. It's lovely, salty and savoury and satisfies that craving, particularly at a party.

SERVES 6
(AS PART OF A MEZE)

PER SERVING:
CALORIES 188KCAL
FAT 15G
SUGAR 0.6G

350g haloumi cheese, sliced lengthways into 1cm-thick slices

Garlic and Mint Dressing (see page 214), to serve

• • • • •·· • • • ·······• • • ·· • • • ·········· • • • ·····• • • ·····• • • ··

Preheat the oven to 200°C/gas 6.

Place the haloumi slices in a single layer on a baking tray. Bake in the preheated oven for 15 minutes, or until lightly browned.

Serve hot with the garlic and mint dressing.

Thai Pork Cups

When I was in Thailand I was thrown into the wonderful world of the Thai flavour profile – sweet, sour, salty, and hot. I just couldn't get enough of it and still to this day I try and season my food in this way. I find that when I hit this flavour profile in food I feel satisfied and full more quickly. These pork cups are perfect for parties and every time I've cooked these for a party, they are the first things to be devoured.

**SERVES 8
(AS PART OF A MEZE)**

PER SERVING:
CALORIES 85KCAL
FAT 2G
SUGAR 3G

50g rice (basmati works best)
2 garlic cloves, grated
1 tbsp grated (peeled) fresh root ginger
2 red or green bird's eye chillies, finely chopped (seeds left in if you like it hot)
large handful of freshly chopped coriander (stalks roughly chopped and leaves finely chopped)
200g lean pork tenderloin, trimmed of fat

1 tbsp vegetable oil
2 shallots, finely chopped
1 tbsp shrimp paste
2 tbsp fish sauce
juice of 2 limes
1 tbsp unrefined dark muscovado sugar
10 mint leaves, finely chopped
8 leaves of Little Gem lettuce, to serve
chopped spring onions, to garnish

• •

Heat a wok over a high heat, add the rice and dry-fry for around 3 minutes until it has browned, shaking the pan a bit. Remove from the heat and lightly pound the rice using a pestle and mortar, then set aside for the garnish.

Using the same pestle and mortar, lightly pound together the garlic, ginger, chillies and coriander stalks (not the leaves) to make a rough paste. Set aside.

Using a heavy, sharp knife, chop the pork tenderloin into small pieces, then chop vigorously to form mince. This is a Thai technique to turn good-quality meat into mince. You can just use lean pork mince but the quality won't be as good and it will be higher in fat.

Heat the oil in the wok over a high heat, add the paste and stir-fry for 3 minutes. Add the minced pork and stir-fry for about 5 minutes, or until the meat is browned. Add the shallots, shrimp paste, fish sauce, lime juice and sugar and stir-fry for a further 2–3 minutes.

Remove from the heat and toss through the chopped coriander leaves and mint. Serve in the lettuce leaf 'cups' and garnish with the toasted rice and the spring onions sprinkled over.

Hara Bhara Kebab

These North Indian kebabs usually resemble green patties, and they get their name from the spinach used in them. These delicious little snacks are traditionally made using ordinary potatoes, but I've replaced them with sweet potatoes as they are high in fibre and are a great source of vitamin E, and I think the sweetness really complements the mix of spices.

MAKES 15 KEBABS

PER KEBAB:
CALORIES 65KCAL
FAT NONE
SUGAR 4G

3 medium-sized sweet potatoes
100g frozen petit pois
200g fresh spinach
2 green chillies, chopped
5cm piece of fresh root ginger, peeled and grated
2 tbsp finely chopped coriander
1 tbsp chaat masala (see Note page 213)
2 tbsp cornflour
salt, to taste

• •

Cook the sweet potatoes whole in their skins in a pan of boiling water for 15 minutes until tender. Add the petit pois to the pan for the last 2 minutes. Drain well and set aside to cool. Meanwhile, rinse the spinach leaves, place them in a separate pan (with just the water that clings to their leaves), cover and cook for 3 minutes, or until wilted. Drain well, pressing out excess water with the back of a spoon. Leave the vegetables to cool, then peel off and discard the sweet potato skins.

Put the sweet potato flesh, peas and spinach into a food processor with all the remaining ingredients and blitz to form a smooth, thick paste. Divide the mixture into 15 equal portions. Shape each portion into a ball and then gently press it between your palms to make a flattened round.

Heat a large frying pan over a medium to high heat until hot, add the kebabs and cook for around 3 minutes on each side, or until browned. You may need to cook them in a few batches.

Serve hot with Raita with Pomegranate and Mint (see page 213).

Japanese Turkey Meatballs

Japanese *tsukune* meatballs are usually made with chicken and pork, but here I've made them lighter using turkey, which is lower in fat. They are so flavourful and make a unique party snack, with hardly any preparation needed.

MAKES 20 MEATBALLS

PER MEATBALL:
CALORIES 85KCAL
FAT NONE
SUGAR 4G

2 dried shiitake mushrooms
500g lean minced turkey
200g panko breadcrumbs
1 egg white
2 tbsp finely chopped
    spring onions
4 garlic cloves, grated
7.5cm piece of fresh root
    ginger, peeled and grated
2 tsp cornflour
1 tsp clear honey
½ tsp salt
½ tsp freshly ground
    black pepper
1 quantity of Soy and Ginger
    Glaze (see page 216)
mixed salad leaves, to serve

Put the shiitake mushrooms in a bowl, cover with hot water and leave to soak for 30 minutes. Drain well, then finely chop.

Combine all the ingredients (except the glaze and salad leaves) in a large bowl, mixing well. Divide the mixture into 20 pieces and roll each into a meatball about the size of a fresh apricot.

Place on a baking tray lined with parchment paper, cover with clingfilm and chill in the fridge for at least 1 hour or overnight. Remove from the fridge and bring to room temperature before cooking.

Preheat the oven to 220°C/gas 7.

Remove the clingfilm from the tray of meatballs and cook them in the preheated oven for 15 minutes. Remove from the oven and carefully brush all over with some of the glaze, then cook for a further 5 minutes until browned.

Serve the meatballs with the remaining glaze in a bowl alongside as a dipping condiment, and accompany with salad leaves.

Uttapam INDIAN DAHL PANCAKES

These are the perfect gluten-free alternative to pancakes (see photograph page 124). Packed full of heat from chillies, they are great served as canapés or finger food. You can make them really small, the size of blini, but that requires a bit of patience. I tend to make uttapam in advance, then leave them to cool, wrap in foil and store in the fridge. Before serving, bring them to room temperature, then reheat in the foil in a preheated oven at 200°C/gas 6 for about 3 minutes to soften and warm them through. Alternatively, remove the foil, place the uttapam on a plate and ping for a few seconds on High in a microwave.

MAKES 12 PANCAKES

PER PANCAKE:
CALORIES 85KCAL
FAT 1G
SUGAR 1G

150g rice flour
100g gram flour
2 tbsp cumin seeds
2 tomatoes, seeded and
    finely chopped
2 green chillies, finely chopped
handful of finely chopped
    coriander
1 tsp baking powder
salt, to taste

• •

Combine all the ingredients in a mixing bowl, then gradually add enough cold water to create a thick batter of dropping consistency.

Heat a frying pan over a medium to high heat until hot. Ladle in some batter to create small pancakes about 5cm in diameter (you'll need to cook these in batches). When bubbles appear on the surface and the batter is set (about 2 minutes), turn the pancakes over and cook the other side for a further 2 minutes. Transfer to a plate, cover with foil and keep warm while you cook the rest.

Serve hot with Coconut Chutney (see page 215).

Mini Poppadums with Sour Apple Chutney

Every time I go for an Indian meal I tell myself to stay away from the poppadums, and every time I am unsuccessful! I am a sucker for savoury and salty snacks and if presented with a big plate piled high with poppadums, it's more likely that I'll eat those than my actual meal. Now typically poppadums are deep-fried to attain that crispy texture, but by experimenting with lighter ways of cooking, I found a great way to still enjoy this snack that is kinder to the waistline, by the magic of the microwave! If you can't find small poppadums at the supermarket, you can do this with big uncooked poppadums too. (See photograph page 134.)

MAKES 20

PER POPPADUM:
CALORIES 58KCAL
FAT 3G
SUGAR 1G

1 Granny Smith eating apple, cored (peel left on), plus 1 Granny Smith (peel left on), cored and thinly sliced, to garnish
1 tbsp desiccated coconut
½ tsp hot chilli powder
½ tsp ground turmeric
1 tbsp freshly chopped coriander
1 tbsp freshly chopped mint leaves
20 mini cumin poppadums
100g cooked fresh white crabmeat
salt

• •

Put the apple, desiccated coconut, chilli powder, turmeric, chopped herbs and salt to taste in a small hand blender/chopper and blitz until combined to make a sour apple 'chutney'.

Place 8 or so mini poppadums on a plate and ping for 10 seconds on High in a microwave oven. Leave to cool on the plate. Continue with the remaining poppadums in the same way until they are all cooked and cool.

To serve, place a small amount of crabmeat onto each poppadum and top with some of the sour apple chutney. Garnish with apple slices and serve.

Mauritian Soured Fruit

In Mauritius, you'll see beach shacks scattered along the shoreline selling anything from ice cream to fried rice and octopus sandwiches. At these shacks you'll also have vendors who specialise in selling bags of these pickled and soured fruits. It sounds odd to have soured pickled fruits that are hot and sweet as a snack on the beach, but the chilli and sourness refreshes you unlike any ice cream! Recently when I was in Mauritius, I devoured a bag of these sweet and sour fruits then jumped straight into the sea. This is the perfect nibble to begin a meal as it opens up your taste buds and has a quite memorable flavour that is unexpected. (See photograph page 134.)

**SERVES 6
(AS PART OF A MEZE)**

PER SERVING:
CALORIES 68KCAL
FAT NONE
SUGAR 15G

250g (prepared weight) mixed unripe mango, unripe papaya and Granny Smith eating apple, peeled, stoned/seeded/cored and cut into pieces
2 tbsp unrefined light muscovado sugar
2 tbsp white wine vinegar
2 tsp tamarind paste
1 tsp Kashmiri chilli powder
100ml apple juice

· ·

Put the pieces of fruit into a bowl, add the sugar, vinegar, tamarind paste and chilli powder and mix together. Cover and leave to marinate in the fridge for 1 hour.

Just before serving, stir in the apple juice. Thread the fruit onto skewers and arrange on a platter (along with the juices) for everyone to enjoy.

Baked Harissa Falafel

Falafel is my ultimate street food, and I love to eat them freshly cooked and burning hot (I never ever seem to learn that I need to let them cool a little before I devour them!). I suppose falafel are to the Arabs what the hamburger is to the Americans in terms of fast food. You can serve them with a wide range of pickled vegetables such as cabbage and radish, along with home-made tahini dressing (see the Endive and Pomegranate with Tahini recipe on page 70 for the dressing). My falafels have the satisfyingly moreish taste but are healthier to eat than the usual fried falafels, as they are oven-baked to get a crispy outer edge.

MAKES 20 FALAFEL

PER FALAFEL:
CALORIES 45KCAL
FAT 1G
SUGAR 1G

1 large white Spanish onion, cut into quarters
6 garlic cloves, peeled
large handful of parsley
1 tbsp Harissa (see page 212)
2 x 400g tins chickpeas, drained and rinsed
2 tbsp ground coriander
2 tbsp ground cumin
1 tsp bicarbonate of soda
salt, to taste

• •

Preheat the oven to 200°C/gas 6. Line a baking tray with parchment paper, brush with a little oil and set aside.

Put all the ingredients into a food processor and blitz until smooth and well mixed.

Using a bowl of cold water, wet your hands and then take a heaped tablespoon of the mixture and roll it into a ball. Place the ball on the baking tray. Repeat with the remaining mixture to make 15–20 falafel.

Bake in the preheated oven for about 10 minutes until golden brown. Serve hot.

Tandoori King Prawns with Mustard Seeds and Cucumber

Tandoori is typically associated with using a tandoor, an Asian cylindrical clay or metal oven, as the method of cooking, but here the tandoori paste acts as a marinade to tenderise and permeate flavour deep into the dish. I'm using prawns as they have a mild sweet flavour and absorb the aromatic flavours of the spices and yoghurt. Prawns are naturally low in fat and high in minerals such as zinc. Normally the tandoori mixes you buy in the supermarket have a red colouring in them, but you can achieve a pink colour with the use of Kashmiri chilli powder, which is usually very vibrant and red in colour. You can get Kashmiri chilli powder online or from international food shops.

**SERVES 6
(AS PART OF A MEZE)**

PER SERVING:
CALORIES 62KCAL
FAT 1G
SUGAR 2G

16 raw king prawns, shelled and deveined but heads and tails left on
1 medium cucumber, sliced in half lengthways, seeded and cut into half moon-shaped slices
1 tbsp black mustard seeds

FOR THE TANDOORI MARINADE
250g 0%-fat Greek-style yoghurt
2 garlic cloves, grated
thumb-sized piece of fresh root ginger, peeled and grated
juice of ½ lemon
1 tbsp ground coriander
1 tbsp ground cumin
1 tsp Kashmiri chilli powder
1 tsp ground turmeric
½ tsp freshly ground black pepper
salt, to taste

• •

Put all the ingredients for the tandoori marinade in a bowl and mix together until combined, then add the prawns and toss to coat all over. Cover and leave to marinate in the fridge for up to 1 hour.

Heat a griddle pan over a high heat until it starts to smoke. Place the prawns straight into the hot pan and leave to cook for 3 minutes on each side until they turn bright pink and start to curl into themselves.

Remove the prawns to a large serving platter, set aside and keep warm.

Quickly add the cucumber slices and mustard seeds to the griddle pan and sauté for a few minutes until the cucumber starts to soften. Scatter them over the prawns and serve warm.

Sizzling Mexican Salmon Cups

This is a beautiful way to spice up salmon using delicious Mexican flavours of lime, cooling avocado and an oomph from fiery jalapeño. It's delicious to serve at a party and so simple to whip up.

**SERVES 6
(AS PART OF A MEZE)**

PER SERVING:
CALORIES 138KCAL
FAT 9G
SUGAR 2G

2 x 120g boneless salmon fillets (skin left on)
1 tsp paprika
2 large tomatoes, seeded and finely diced
1 avocado, halved, stoned, peeled and finely diced
1 red onion, finely diced

½ green jalapeño chilli, finely diced
handful of roughly chopped coriander
juice of 1 lime
salt and freshly ground black pepper
6 cos lettuce leaves, to serve

• •

Preheat the oven to 200°C/gas 6.

Place the salmon in an ovenproof dish, sprinkle with the paprika and cook in the preheated oven for 15 minutes, or until golden brown and cooked.

Remove from the oven and cool slightly, then remove the skin and carefully break up the salmon into flakes.

Meanwhile, as the salmon is cooling, put the tomatoes, avocado, red onion, jalapeño chilli, coriander, lime juice and seasoning into a mixing bowl and stir to combine. Add the flakes of salmon and mix gently, being careful not to crush the fish flakes.

Spoon equal amounts of the salmon mixture onto the lettuce leaves, then serve.

Kalatini CHICKPEA FLAN

Kalatini is a popular street food found in Northern Morocco and parts of Algeria, and is described as a chickpea flan. Its name, a corruption of the Spanish *caliente* (hot), comes from street vendors shouting out '*caliente, caliente*', meaning 'get it while it's hot'. The first time I came across this dish was in 2013 when a friend was talking about Moroccan street food and I was so intrigued that I had to go home and test it for myself. In my opinion, texturally it is similar to hummus but is milder in taste and slightly firmer.

This is a really versatile dish and takes no time at all to prepare. I love serving this with toasted pitta bread, with a hefty sprinkling of ground cumin and paprika over the top of the kalatini (see photograph page 124). Normally the dish uses roasted chickpeas that are then ground into a flour, but this flour is hard to get hold of or requires a lot of time to make at home, so I've substituted an easier option that is readily available – chickpea flour, also known as besan or gram flour.

SERVES 6
(AS PART OF A MEZE)

PER SERVING:
CALORIES 216KCAL
FAT 11G
SUGAR 1G

200g chickpea/besan/ gram flour
1 tbsp ground cumin
1 tsp paprika
1 tsp salt

2 eggs, beaten
4 tbsp olive oil
toasted pitta bread, torn into pieces, to serve

• •

Preheat the oven to 200°C/gas 6. Grease a baking tray and set aside.

Combine the dry ingredients in a bowl. Whisk together the eggs, oil and 600ml cold water in a jug. Gradually add the egg mixture to the dry ingredients and mix until thoroughly combined and lump-free. Pour the mixture onto the baking tray, making sure it spreads out in an even layer.

Bake in the preheated oven for 35–40 minutes until the kalatini is browned on top and set with a slight wobble.

Remove from the oven and leave to cool a little, then let guests dip toasted pitta into the warm mixture. Offer ground cumin, paprika and home-made harissa (see page 212) as side condiments to this dish.

Lychee and Tuna Ceviche

The most important thing about making a ceviche, a tangy dish of raw cured fish, at home is to use the freshest fish you can get hold of. Once you've added the acidic element to the dish, the tuna needs only 20 minutes of marinating; any more and the fish will become watery and tough. The fresh tastes, and allowing the fish flavour to sing through, are the keys to a good ceviche.

I had this combination of tuna and lychees on the beach in Mauritius and I remember being so shocked at how well the two paired together; the mellow, sweet and floral dimension of the lychees adds so many layers to the ceviche. This is perfect for entertaining on a long summer's night or when you want the sun to come out! (See photograph page 134.)

**SERVES 10
(AS PART OF A MEZE)**

PER SERVING:
CALORIES 51KCAL
FAT 1G
SUGAR 4G

250g good-quality fresh skinless and boneless tuna loin, trimmed
1 banana shallot, peeled
10 tinned lychees, drained, but reserve 2 tbsp lychee syrup from the tin

2 tbsp finely snipped chives
1 tbsp rice wine vinegar
½ tsp black mustard seeds
pinch of salt
pinch of freshly ground black pepper

. . . .

Finely chop the tuna, shallot and lychees and mix together in a bowl. Add all the remaining ingredients and stir to mix. Cover and chill in the fridge for 20 minutes before serving.

Spoon into shot glasses and serve.

Temari Salmon Balls with Sticky Soy Glaze

These balls of smoked salmon 'sushi' are really easy to prepare and are light and refreshing for a party. You can make this recipe ahead of time and leave in the fridge – the temari balls will keep for up to 24 hours once they are made. Perfect served with the Soy and Ginger Glaze (see page 216). (See also photograph page 134.)

MAKES 15 BALLS

PER BALL (INCLUDING SOY GLAZE):
CALORIES 27KCAL
FAT 1G
SUGAR NONE

100g cold cooked sushi rice
2 tbsp black sesame seeds
wasabi paste, to taste
120g smoked salmon, thinly sliced

chives, to garnish
Soy and Ginger Glaze (see page 216), to serve

• •

Mix the sushi rice and sesame seeds together. With wet hands, roll 1 heaped tablespoon of sushi rice into a ball. Continue rolling balls of sushi rice in the same way until you have used up all the rice mixture (it will make around 15 balls).

Place a little wasabi paste on the top of each sushi ball. Wrap smoked salmon around each one so that it covers the ball and wasabi paste. Top each temari with a criss-cross of chives to garnish.

Set the sushi balls on a serving dish with the soy and ginger glaze served as a dipping sauce in a bowl placed in the centre.

CELEBRATION FOOD

'Pack flavour into food using fresh ingredients like fresh herbs and spices, citrus fruit juices and chillies, and use the natural sugars found in fruit to add sweetness.'

CELEBRATION FOOD

As a sociable family- and friend-orientated kind of girl, I am a great lover of hosting fabulous, informal dinners where my guests leave feeling full and happy. I love having people over for dinner just as much as I enjoy hosting parties.

The thing that makes me smile the most is preparing food that I can share with my friends and family around a dining table. It's informal, messy and noisy, and food shared in this way creates warm memories of time spent together.

My one-pots, lunch recipes and nibbles are all great for sharing with friends but in this chapter I want to focus on food that looks impressive as well as tasting delicious. These are dishes you can easily whip up, that look stunning on the plate but don't leave you with any guilt or feeling as though you're in a food coma afterwards!

Chinese Chilli Prawns with Bamboo Shoots

A twist on the classic sweet and sour, this recipe is a fresher, tastier and healthier version of your takeaway nights. So treat yourself without guilt and save yourself a trip to your local Chinese.

SERVES 4

PER SERVING:
CALORIES 110KCAL
FAT 3G
SUGAR 3G

1 tbsp vegetable oil
4 garlic cloves, finely chopped
1–2 red chillies, finely chopped
5cm piece of fresh root ginger, peeled and finely chopped
300g (prepared weight) raw king prawns, shelled and deveined
1 x 225g tin bamboo shoots, drained and rinsed

2 tbsp tomato ketchup
2 tbsp light soy sauce
1 tbsp shaoxing wine
200ml boiling water
juice of 1 lime
3 spring onions, finely chopped, to garnish

. . . .

Heat the oil in a wok or a heavy-based frying pan over a high heat, add the garlic, chillies and ginger and stir-fry for 30 seconds. Add the prawns along with the bamboo shoots, tomato ketchup, soy sauce, shaoxing wine and boiling water and simmer for 2 minutes.

Add the lime juice and then remove from the heat. You don't want to overcook the prawns.

Garnish with spring onions and serve with steamed brown rice.

Baked Sea Bass with Pink Peppercorns

This is a celebration dish, and its beauty lies in having a wonderful large baked sea bass resting on a bed of beautiful Kale and Sumac Tabbouleh (see page 66). It creates the perfect centrepiece.

SERVES 4

PER SERVING:
CALORIES 265KCAL
FAT 15G
SUGAR NONE

1 x 1.2–1.3kg whole sea bass, gutted and scaled
bunch of freshly chopped coriander (including stalks)
bunch of freshly chopped parsley (including stalks)
2 garlic cloves, finely chopped
1 tbsp fennel seeds, lightly toasted (see page 17)
1 tsp ground turmeric
1 tsp white pepper
pinch of salt

2 tbsp olive oil
Kale and Sumac Tabbouleh (see page 66), to serve

FOR THE DRESSING
2 tbsp olive oil
juice of 2 limes
2 tbsp freshly chopped parsley
1 tbsp pink peppercorns, crushed
pinch of salt

Preheat the oven to 180°C/gas 4.

Clean the sea bass, wiping it inside and out with kitchen paper. Use a sharp knife to gently score the fish with 3–4 diagonal cuts on both sides. Stuff the inside of the fish with the coriander and parsley.

Mix together the garlic, toasted fennel seeds, ground spices and salt and rub all over the outside of the fish. Place the fish on a baking tray, then drizzle over the oil.

Bake in the preheated oven for 30 minutes until the skin is crispy. Check if the fish is cooked – the flesh should be opaque and feel firm to the touch. Return to the oven for a further 5 minutes if necessary.

Meanwhile, whisk together all the dressing ingredients until completely combined. Once the fish is cooked, carefully transfer it to the bed of tabbouleh. Drizzle the dressing over the fish and serve.

Sea Bream with Chermoula

Chermoula is a fragrant mix of spices and herbs used across North Africa, namely Tunisia, Algeria and Morocco. The blend varies quite a lot from country to country and region to region, but generally the staple elements include garlic, olive oil and lemon and it is most often used to season fish. I remember being in a fishing village called Essaouira in Morocco and I tasted the most beautiful sardines, they had a chermoula rub and were grilled directly over a BBQ – the best sardines I've ever eaten. Since then, I've always liked to prepare my fish with a chermoula rub, particularly with sardines but also with sea bream. Here, I'm using sea bream as it holds its shape better and really absorbs the wonderful flavours of this chermoula.

SERVES 4

PER SERVING:
CALORIES 210KCAL
FAT 10G
SUGAR NONE

1 x 1.2–1.3kg whole sea bream, gutted and scaled
3 garlic cloves, peeled
4 tbsp finely chopped coriander leaves
3 tbsp finely chopped parsley
2 tbsp extra virgin olive oil
zest and juice of 1 lemon
2 tsp cumin seeds, ground
2 tsp paprika
½ tsp white pepper

Preheat the oven to 180°C/gas 4.

Clean the sea bream, wiping it inside and out with kitchen paper. Use a sharp knife to gently score the fish with 3–4 diagonal cuts on both sides.

Using a pestle and mortar or a food processor, crush or blitz all the remaining ingredients together until you get a vivid green paste (chermoula). Rub the chermoula all over the skin, into the slashes and into the cavity of the fish.

Place the fish on a baking tray and bake in the preheated oven for about 30 minutes, or until cooked all the way through.

Carefully transfer to a serving plate and serve with Lime and Mustard Rice with Curry Leaves (see page 101).

3 Pepper Pork Stir-fry

This recipe is reserved for those times when you can't plan when your family and friends are going to show up. It uses a lot of storecupboard spices and you can create a mouth-watering stir-fry in less than 20 minutes.

SERVES 4

PER SERVING:
CALORIES 510KCAL
FAT 11G
SUGAR 8G

80g cornflour
1½ tsp white pepper
1 pork tenderloin (about 300g), trimmed of fat and finely sliced
1 tbsp sesame oil
2 garlic cloves, grated
1 tbsp grated (peeled) fresh root ginger
2 large carrots, peeled and cut into matchsticks (julienned)
175g mixed baby corn and mangetout
1 lemon grass stalk, trimmed and bruised
1 tbsp pink peppercorns, ground
1 tbsp Sichuan peppercorns, ground
3 tbsp dark soy sauce
3 tbsp oyster sauce
250g pack dried medium egg noodles
chopped spring onions and freshly chopped coriander leaves, to garnish

• •

In a bowl, mix the cornflour with the white pepper. Roll the pork tenderloin slices in the mixture, coating them evenly, then shake off any excess.

Heat the oil in a large wok over a medium heat, add the pork and stir-fry until browned all over. Add all the remaining ingredients (except the egg noodles and garnish) and stir-fry for a further 4–5 minutes, or until the pork is cooked and the vegetables are tender.

Meanwhile, cook the egg noodles in a large pan of boiling water for 3–4 minutes (or according to packet instructions) until just cooked or al dente. Drain well.

To serve, divide the noodles between 4 plates, then arrange the pork and vegetable stir-fry on top (discard the lemon grass stalk). Garnish with spring onions and coriander sprinkled over.

Braised Chicken with Tamarind and Pak Choi

My fondness for pak choi and Chinese cabbage led me to create this beautiful, aromatic and healthy Asian-inspired casserole.

SERVES 4

PER SERVING:
CALORIES 312KCAL
FAT 13G
SUGAR 10G

4 chicken quarters, skinned and fat trimmed
1 tbsp vegetable oil
2 onions, thickly sliced
1 tbsp coriander seeds, coarsely crushed
1 tbsp tamarind paste
1 rounded tbsp tomato purée

700ml vegetable stock
3 medium tomatoes, quartered
2 pak choi, trimmed and halved
salt and freshly ground black pepper
freshly chopped coriander, to garnish

Season the chicken quarters with salt and pepper. Heat the oil in a sauté pan with a lid (or a shallow, lidded casserole) over a medium to high heat and fry the chicken for 5–10 minutes until golden, turning occasionally.

Transfer the chicken to a plate and keep to one side. You will need about 1 tablespoon of fat left in the pan for cooking the onions, so drain off the excess.

Add the onions to the pan and cook until they have a little colour and are beginning to soften, stirring occasionally. Add the coriander seeds and cook for a minute or two to release the flavour in the spice. Stir in the tamarind paste and tomato purée, then pour in the stock.

Return the chicken to the pan along with the tomatoes and bring to a simmer. Cover and continue to cook, allowing the sauce to just simmer for about 1 hour, or until the meat is completely tender, stirring occasionally.

Remove the lid and skim off any excess fat from the surface of the sauce, then add the pak choi and simmer for a further 2–3 minutes to soften it. Scatter over the chopped coriander to garnish and serve.

Thai-style Grilled Lobster

Lobster has always been thought of as a luxury meal, but that doesn't mean you have to be cautious with it and dress it in the classic way. Lobster is so versatile and can really withstand the punchy and powerful flavour of this Thai dressing, without losing any of its natural flavours of the sea. Perfect for a romantic night in or a special occasion.

SERVES 2

PER SERVING:
CALORIES 257KCAL
FAT 4G
SUGAR 9G

1 large lobster (about 1kg), pre-cooked and cold
juice of 2 limes
1½ tsp tamarind paste
3 garlic cloves, peeled
1 thumb-size piece of fresh galangal or fresh root ginger, peeled and sliced
½ red pepper, seeded and diced
1–2 red chillies, finely chopped (seeded if you prefer less heat)
2 tbsp fish sauce
1 heaped tsp unrefined light muscovado sugar
large bunch of freshly chopped coriander (including stalks)
salt, to taste

• •

Preheat the grill to high.

Cut the lobster in half lengthways then put the halves flesh-side up on a baking tray and set aside.

Put all the remaining ingredients into a food processor with enough cold water to loosen the dressing and blitz to make a thin paste, then pour it evenly over the lobster.

Grill for 6–8 minutes, or until the lobster is lightly charred and golden. Serve on its own or with a simple green salad.

Hot Pot

There are many different variants and origins of hot pot across Japan, China and Korea. Here, I'm taking the basic idea of having a really good base stock and enjoying this with friends around the table. Conceptually, it's like preparing a fondue, and once the preparation is done, you can place it all onto the table and everyone gets stuck in. It's a really fun way to share a meal with friends and family.

SERVES 6

PER SERVING:
CALORIES 39KCAL
FAT 1G
SUGAR 2G

FOR THE SOUP BASE
1.4 litres vegetable stock
5 dried shiitake mushrooms
1 star anise
10 Sichuan peppercorns
1 tbsp Sriracha (see page 219)
2 spring onions, roughly
    chopped
2.5cm piece of fresh root ginger
    (peel on), washed and sliced
pinch each of salt and
    white pepper

TO SERVE
(you can serve as many or
    as few of the following
    ingredients as you wish,
    depending on the number
    of guests; using up leftover
    raw vegetables from the
    fridge works just as well too)
lean sirloin steak, thinly sliced
mixed fresh mushrooms, sliced
Chinese cabbage, shredded
beansprouts
pak choi, halved (with stalk
    left on)
watercress
freshly chopped coriander
    and freshly torn basil leaves
lime wedges

• •

To make the soup base, place all the ingredients in a pan. Bring to the boil, then reduce the heat and simmer, uncovered, for around 20 minutes to enable all the flavours to infuse. Adjust the seasoning to taste.

To serve, arrange the steak, mushrooms, cabbage, beansprouts, greens and herbs on separate plates. Transfer the soup base to a camping stove or fondue and set it up in the centre of the table. Guests can then help themselves and dip their meat and vegetables into the broth. Squeeze over lime juice to taste.

Alternatively, you can serve up the hot soup base into bowls and guests can then place their meat and vegetables directly into their own bowls.

Beef Bulgogi

Bulgogi is a really popular Korean beef dish. It's usually made from thinly sliced beef marinated in a mixture of soy sauce, black pepper, spring onions and sugar for 2–3 hours to enhance the flavour of the meat and to make it really tender. Traditionally bulgogi is then griddled and served with leafy vegetables, some kimchi (like my Brussels Sprout Kimchi on page 218) and dipping sauces alongside, but it's equally delicious served with rice and kimchi, the choice is yours.

SERVES 4

PER SERVING:
CALORIES 290KCAL
FAT 12G
SUGAR 11G

600g lean sirloin steak (trimmed of fat), thinly sliced
100ml light soy sauce
2 garlic cloves, minced
3 tbsp mirin
1 tbsp sesame oil
1 tbsp unrefined light muscovado sugar
2 spring onions, finely chopped
1 tsp freshly ground black pepper
iceberg or Romaine lettuce leaves, to serve

Put all the ingredients (except the lettuce) in a bowl and mix together, then leave to marinate in the fridge for 2–3 hours.

Remove from the fridge and let the mixture come up to room temperature.

Heat a griddle pan over a high heat until it is searing hot and smoking, add the beef slices and marinade, and cook for a minute or so on each side until the beef is nicely browned.

Transfer to a serving dish. Serve with iceberg or Romaine lettuce, Brussels Sprout Kimchi (see page 218) and some Sriracha (see page 219).

Djaj Mhamar

ROASTED MOROCCAN CHICKEN WITH GREEN OLIVES

This is a really nice change from a traditional roast chicken. It starts as a one-pot dish and the beauty is that all the work goes in right at the beginning, then it's just a case of letting it do its thing and allowing the flavours to meld and infuse together. This is delicious served with a green salad.

SERVES 6

PER SERVING:
CALORIES 258KCAL
FAT 15G
SUGAR 2G

1 onion, puréed or very
    finely chopped
3 garlic cloves, puréed or
    finely crushed
a pinch of saffron strands
1 tsp white pepper
1 tsp ground cinnamon
1 tsp ground ginger
1 tsp ground turmeric

2 tbsp freshly chopped coriander
2 tbsp freshly chopped parsley
1 cinnamon stick
zest and juice of 1 lemon
1 x 1.2kg whole chicken, skin
    removed and fat trimmed
150g green olives
salt

• •

Preheat the oven to 180°C/gas 4.

Put all the ingredients (except the chicken and green olives) in a roasting dish and mix together, seasoning with salt to taste. Add the chicken and massage the mixture thoroughly into the bird, then scatter the olives around.

Add 300ml cold water to the dish, then roast in the preheated oven for 1¼–1½ hours, or until the chicken is cooked all the way through.

To serve, place the chicken on a big serving plate and spoon over all the sauce.

Pork Medallions with Smashed Cucumber

Smashing cucumbers is a popular Chinese method that allows the cucumber to absorb the flavours of the salad dressing. The biggest tip when cooking pork tenderloin is to make sure it doesn't dry out, as it is a lean cut of pork. In this recipe, the pork is wrapped in foil so it steams in its own juices and retains all of its wonderful flavour.

SERVES 4

PER SERVING:
CALORIES 135KCAL
FAT 3G
SUGAR 2G

400g pork tenderloin
1 tbsp fennel seeds
2 tbsp freshly chopped parsley
zest of 1 lemon (save the juice
    for the salad)
1 garlic clove, grated
salt and freshly ground
    black pepper

FOR THE SALAD
1 cucumber
¼ medium red onion,
    finely chopped
2 spring onions, finely chopped
1 large red chilli, seeded and
    finely chopped (leave seeds
    in if you like the heat)
juice of 1 lemon
2 tsp rice wine vinegar
½ tsp white pepper

• •

Preheat the oven to 160°C/gas 2½.

Clean the tenderloin and remove as much of the sinew and fat as possible. Slice the pork in half lengthways, being careful not to completely cut it in half, just enough to insert the stuffing. Stuff the tenderloin with the fennel seeds, parsley, lemon zest and garlic and season with salt and pepper.

Wrap in foil, place on a baking tray and cook in the preheated oven for 30 minutes until cooked all the way through. Remove from the oven and leave to rest for 10–15 minutes.

While the meat is resting, make the salad. Cut the cucumber in half lengthways and remove the seeds. Smash each cucumber half with the side of a knife until it's flattened and then cut into 2cm slices. Put the cucumber in a bowl along with all the other salad ingredients and mix, adding a little salt to taste.

Unwrap the pork and slice into medallions. Serve with the mixed salad alongside.

Cod with Almonds and Saffron

This dish is so easy to prepare that once you've got everything ready to go into the pot, you can get yourself ready and not have to worry about spending time slaving away in the kitchen. The flavours are so subtle, and this works really well with Griddled Sweet Potatoes with Mint, Chilli and Smoked Garlic (see page 68).

SERVES 4

PER SERVING:
CALORIES 326KCAL
FAT 12G
SUGAR 6G

700g skinless and boneless cod
   fillets, cut into large chunks
600ml fish or vegetable stock
pinch of saffron strands
1 tbsp olive oil
1 onion, finely chopped
3 garlic cloves, finely chopped
1 tbsp ground cumin
1 tbsp ground coriander
½ cinnamon stick

1 tbsp tomato purée
3 plum tomatoes, quartered
2 tbsp ground almonds
zest of 1 lemon
small bunch of freshly
   chopped coriander
handful of toasted flaked
   almonds
salt and freshly ground
   black pepper

• • • • • · · · • • • · • · · • • · · • · • • • · · • • · · • • • · · • • • · · · • • •

Season the fish chunks with salt and pepper and set to one side.

Heat the stock in a pan until it is simmering, then add the saffron. Remove from the heat and let it steep for a few minutes.

Meanwhile, heat the oil in a casserole or heavy-based pan over a medium heat, add the onion and garlic and cook for a few minutes until soft, being careful not to burn the garlic. Add the cumin, coriander, cinnamon stick and tomato purée and cook for a few minutes until the mixture just starts to stick to the pan. Add the tomatoes and cook for a few more minutes until the tomatoes start to soften.

Add the ground almonds, lemon zest and saffron-infused stock, then add the seasoned fish chunks, making sure they are fully immersed in the sauce. Bring to a simmer and simmer, uncovered, for 10–12 minutes until the fish is cooked and tender.

Check and adjust the seasoning to taste. Stir in the chopped coriander, scatter with the flaked almonds and serve.

Beef with Lemon Grass and Sichuan Pepper

An alternative and exciting way to enjoy your steak, mixed with fragrant lemon grass and vermicelli noodles, this dish is perfect for feeding the family during the week but looks good enough to serve to friends too. Any leftovers can be packed away for a tasty lunch the next day.

SERVES 4

PER SERVING:
CALORIES 340KCAL
FAT 10G
SUGAR NONE

150g dried rice vermicelli noodles
1 tbsp vegetable oil
4 garlic cloves, finely chopped
3cm piece of fresh root ginger, peeled and chopped
1 lemon grass stalk, trimmed and finely chopped
1 long red chilli, finely chopped
500g lean sirloin steak (trimmed of fat), thinly sliced
1 tbsp Sichuan pepper
2 tbsp fish sauce
4 spring onions, coarsely chopped
handful each of freshly chopped or torn basil, coriander and mint leaves
juice of 1 lime

Place the noodles in a heatproof bowl, cover with boiling water and leave to soak for around 5 minutes (or according to packet instructions) until tender, then drain and cool.

Heat the oil in a wok over a high heat, add the garlic, ginger, lemon grass and chilli and stir-fry for 30 seconds. Add the beef and Sichuan pepper and stir-fry for few minutes, or until the beef is browned all over – you don't want to overcook it.

Add the fish sauce, toss in the noodles, spring onions and herbs, then remove from the heat.

Turn out onto a big platter, squeeze over the lime juice and serve.

Chicken Bastilla

Bastilla, b'stilla and pastilla are different spellings for the same Moroccan dish: in essence, a meat pie made with warqa pastry (a thin, filo-like pastry) with a savoury and sweet flavour. I have to be honest, I was never a fan of meat with sweet flavours, but I was converted when I first tasted a bastilla on holiday in Morocco. It was a pigeon bastilla heady with spice, contrasting with a sweet fruity mixture and a sticky top to the pastry. I think this is a really lovely dish to put together and present to guests, as it creates a great centrepiece and you can serve it with a simple fresh green salad along side.

SERVES 8

PER SERVING:
CALORIES 245KCAL
FAT 5G
SUGAR 8G

100g couscous
175ml boiling water
1 tsp olive oil
1 large Spanish onion, finely diced
2 garlic cloves, grated
1 tbsp ground cumin
1 tsp ground turmeric
60g sultanas

250g leftover cold roast chicken meat (skin removed), torn into small pieces
5–6 large sheets of filo pastry
1 tbsp toasted flaked almonds
1 heaped tsp unrefined icing sugar
½ tsp ground cinnamon
salt and freshly ground black pepper

• •

Preheat the oven to 180°C/gas 4. Grease a shallow 20cm round cake tin with oil and line with parchment paper. Set aside.

Put the couscous into a heatproof bowl. Pour over the boiling water and stir. Cover with clingfilm and leave to stand for 5 minutes until all the liquid has been absorbed. Fluff up the grains with a fork.

Heat the oil in a frying pan over a medium to high heat. Add the onion, garlic, ground spices and sultanas and cook until the onion begins to soften, making sure you don't burn the spices – you can always add a tablespoon or so of water if the pan becomes too dry.

Remove from the heat and tip the onion mixture into a large bowl. Add the chicken and soaked couscous and season with salt and pepper. Set to one side.

Place 3–4 sheets of filo into the cake tin, overlapping them so they cover the base and up the sides of the tin, letting the edges drape over the rim.

Now, using the cake tin as your guide, you will need to cut out 2 circles (the same circumference as the tin) from the remaining 2 sheets of filo – these will be placed on the top (once cooked, they will in fact form the base of the bastilla).

Spoon the couscous mixture evenly into the filo-lined tin. Place the 2 circles of filo over the top, then fold in the draped edges of filo over the top to form a neat, sealed bastilla.

Bake in the preheated oven for around 25–30 minutes, or until golden in colour and crisp.

Remove from the oven and leave to cool slightly before turning out. Place a serving plate over the top of the tin, then carefully turn it upside-down and turn the bastilla out onto the plate. Sprinkle over the flaked almonds, then dust the top with the icing sugar and cinnamon. Serve with a green salad and some home-made harissa and yoghurt dressing (see Note below).

NOTE
To make harissa and yoghurt dressing, combine 3 tbsp low-fat natural yoghurt and 1 tbsp Harissa (see page 212) in a small bowl.

Spicy Whole Roasted Cauliflower

You don't have to be a vegetarian to absolutely love this dish. We can tend to forget how flavoursome vegetables can be, particularly cauliflower, the king of vegetables. Roasted in the oven with a layering of spice, this is a knockout dish and you will be amazed at how much you enjoy it.

SERVES 4

PER SERVING:
CALORIES 106KCAL
FAT 2G
SUGAR 6G

1 large cauliflower (left whole), base trimmed and leaves removed
100g 0%-fat Greek-style yoghurt
1 tbsp mild madras curry powder
1 tsp ground cumin
1 tsp paprika
1 tsp freshly ground black pepper
salt, to taste
Garlic and Mint Dressing (see page 214), to serve

• •

Bring a large pan of water to the boil, then add the whole cauliflower, cover and simmer for 15 minutes. Drain and set aside.

Meanwhile, preheat the oven to 160°C/gas 2½. Line a roasting tray with parchment paper, then lightly rub it with a small amount of oil to prevent the cauliflower from sticking. Set aside.

In small bowl, mix together the yoghurt, curry powder, cumin, paprika and seasoning.

Place the cauliflower in the roasting tray and spoon the yoghurt mixture/marinade all over. Roast in the preheated oven for 45 minutes, or until tender. You can check if the cauliflower is cooked through by inserting a skewer into the centre – it should be soft but still hold its shape. The outside will be slightly charred in colour.

Remove from the oven and leave the cauliflower to rest for 10 minutes before serving. Serve with the garlic and mint dressing and a green salad alongside.

Lamb with Blackened Sweetcorn Salsa

This dish takes me back to summer BBQs and lazy summer afternoons. It's so much more exciting and tasty than your traditional sausages and burgers. You can also achieve the BBQ effect inside on a rainy day by using these fresh, fragrant ingredients and a griddle pan, as I do here.

SERVES 4

PER SERVING:
CALORIES 265KCAL
FAT 11G
SUGAR 3G

4 lean lamb leg steaks
1 tbsp olive oil

FOR THE SWEETCORN SALSA
2 fresh corn cobs, leaves and
  'silk' removed
¼ red onion, finely chopped

2 spring onions, finely chopped
2 tomatoes, finely chopped
1 tbsp freshly chopped mint
  leaves
juice of 1 lemon
pinch of ground cumin
salt and freshly ground
  black pepper

• •

To make the salsa, heat a frying pan over a medium heat until it is hot. Add the corn cobs and cook for about 3 minutes on each side, or until the corn starts to blacken and the pan begins to get sticky. Remove from the heat and leave to cool for around 10 minutes.

Once cooled, carefully drag a sharp knife down the side of the corn cobs to release the kernels. Put the sweetcorn kernels into a mixing bowl, add all the other salsa ingredients and mix together. Season with salt and pepper and set aside.

Heat a griddle pan over a high heat until it is smoking hot. Rub the lamb steaks all over with the oil and season with salt and pepper, then add to the hot pan and cook for 3–4 minutes on each side, turning once.

Remove to a plate, cover with foil and leave to rest for 3–4 minutes. Serve the lamb steaks with the sweetcorn salsa alongside.

Kerala-style Mussels

The wonderful thing about cooking, from the preparation to the sit-down meal, is that it has the ability to transport you to a different place. Mussels do that for me and always remind me of holiday food. These mussels were inspired by a Keralan chef in Mauritius who prepared them for me as he wanted me to sample the sea flavours of his homeland in India.

SERVES 4

PER SERVING:
CALORIES 100KCAL
FAT 7G
SUGAR 1G

5 dried red chillies, soaked in hot water and drained (see page 17)
500g fresh live mussels
1 tsp coconut oil (or vegetable oil)
3 small shallots, sliced
1 tsp garam masala
1 tsp ground turmeric
1 tsp paprika
½ cinnamon stick
2 tsp white wine vinegar
2 tbsp desiccated coconut
salt
fresh curry leaves, to garnish

• •

Grind the drained red chillies to a powder using a pestle and mortar. Set aside.

Clean the mussels well in cold water and remove the beards. Discard any mussels with broken shells or that do not close when firmly tapped with the back of a knife.

Heat the oil in a heavy-based casserole over a medium to high heat, add the shallots and sauté until they soften and caramelise a bit on the edges. Add the ground spices (including the ground chilli) and cinnamon stick and cook for a further 30 seconds, then add the mussels, vinegar, coconut and salt to taste and stir.

Cover tightly with a lid and leave to cook for 5 minutes. The mussels are cooked when their shells have opened – discard any mussels that remain firmly closed. Garnish with curry leaves and serve.

Rabbit with Cumin and Preserved Lemon

Rabbit will always remind me of my dad, as he used to prepare wild rabbit with peas, typically French-style with garlic and thyme. I love rabbit and almost always cook my dad's recipe, but I've also discovered another way of cooking it that is different but still really delicious. I found that preserved lemons work really well in taming the wild gamey flavours of the rabbit. The most important thing to remember is not to overcook the meat as it can toughen very easily because it is so lean – rabbit is a great low-fat meat.

SERVES 4

PER SERVING:
CALORIES 392KCAL
FAT 14G
SUGAR 3G

2 tbsp olive oil
2 rabbits, jointed (ask your butcher to prepare these for you)
1 large red onion, sliced
3 garlic cloves, smashed
1 tbsp ground coriander
1 tbsp cumin seeds
a pinch of saffron strands
300ml chicken stock
2 preserved lemons, drained and sliced
salt and freshly ground black pepper

Heat the oil in a sauté pan over a medium heat, add the rabbit joints and cook until browned on all sides, around 3–4 minutes. Add the red onion and garlic and cook for a few minutes until the onion starts to soften.

Add the spices, stock, preserved lemons and seasoning and bring to a simmer. Cover with a lid and simmer gently over the lowest heat for about 1 hour until the rabbit is tender, stirring occasionally.

Serve with toasted wholemeal pitta bread and a mixed leaf salad.

SWEETS & TREATS

'It's important that you treat yourself every so often so don't hold back on desserts.'

Sweet Apple and Spice Pancakes

These are so easy to whip up that you can get the kids involved and get the kitchen a bit messy in the process! I love cooking with kids as they can learn about healthier food options and start to enjoy the food more.

MAKES 8 SMALL PANCAKES

PER PANCAKE:
CALORIES 154KCAL
FAT 1G
SUGAR 17G

175g wholemeal flour
1 tbsp ground mixed spice
1 tsp baking powder
100g unrefined golden
    caster sugar
2 egg whites
250ml skimmed milk
2 medium eating apples, peeled,
    cored and finely chopped

TO SERVE (OPTIONAL)
low-fat natural yoghurt
mixed fresh berries
agave nectar

Combine the flour, mixed spice and baking powder in a mixing bowl. In a separate bowl, whisk together the sugar and egg whites until light, fluffy and aerated.

Slowly pour the milk into the flour mixture, beating thoroughly to ensure there are no lumps, then stir in the apples. Carefully fold in the whisked egg white mixture.

Heat a pancake pan over a medium to high heat until hot. Place 2 small ladlefuls of the pancake mixture into the pan, allowing it to spread evenly. Cook for 1–2 minutes, or until you see bubbles appearing on the surface and the underside is golden, then carefully flip the pancake over and cook the other side for a few minutes.

Remove the cooked pancake to a plate, cover with foil and keep warm, while you cook the rest of the pancakes in the same way (8 in total).

Serve the pancakes on their own or, if you like, place a tablespoon of yoghurt over each pancake, tumble over some mixed berries, then drizzle with a little agave nectar and serve.

Lemon Verbena and Rose Petal Jellies

Isn't there something warming and magical about jellies?! I guess it's because it takes us all back to our childhoods and the excitement and anticipation of that unique soft sensation in your mouth. I remember whenever there were any parties mum would always add a bowlful of jelly to the table; it's so nostalgic it's making me smile as I write. This jelly is fresh and aromatic and leaves a wonderful perfumed flavour in the mouth.

SERVES 6

PER SERVING:
CALORIES 110KCAL
FAT NONE
SUGAR 25G

6 gelatine sheets
150g unrefined golden
    caster sugar
handful of lemon verbena
    leaves (around 12 leaves),
    plus extra for serving

juice of 1 lemon
1 tbsp rosewater
3 tbsp dried rose petals

• •

Soak the gelatine sheets in cold water for a few minutes to soften (this is called blooming).

Pour 600ml cold water into a pan, add the sugar and heat together until the sugar has dissolved, then remove from the heat.

Squeeze out the excess water from the softened gelatine sheets, add these to the warm sugar syrup and stir until completely dissolved. Stir in the handful of lemon verbena leaves along with the lemon juice and rosewater.

Add the rose petals to the lemon-rosewater mix and leave to soak for a few minutes. Pour the mixture into 6 glasses, dividing it evenly between the glasses.

Leave to cool, then transfer the glasses to the fridge to let the jellies set, around 1½ hours. Serve.

Sweet Potato Halwa

There are variations of halwa across India, Pakistan and the Middle East. The common thing that usually links all these variations together is that they are very sweet, very dense and usually scented with rosewater or perhaps even orange blossom water. In all its guises, halwa is most definitely a celebratory dessert usually reserved for family gatherings, weddings and other festivities. I've taken out a lot of the ingredients that usually make it very dense and rich (such as powdered milk, ghee, butter and sometimes even eggs), and have instead used cooked sweet potato to get that sweet and dense texture without all the extra calories.

SERVES 4

PER SERVING:
CALORIES 284KCAL
FAT 9G
SUGAR 32G

1 tsp olive oil
2 cooked sweet potatoes, peeled and mashed
75g unrefined golden caster sugar
pinch of salt
5 green cardamom pods, crushed
½ tsp rosewater
handful of chopped pistachios
handful of chopped flaked almonds
toasted desiccated coconut and 0%-fat Greek-style yoghurt, to serve (optional)

Heat the oil in a heavy-based pan, add the mashed sweet potato and cook for 3–4 minutes, stirring occasionally. Add the sugar, salt, cardamom and rosewater and cook for a further 4 minutes until the mixture becomes really dry and darker in colour, stirring occasionally.

Remove from the heat, then stir in the pistachios and almonds. Cool the halwa mixture slightly, then spoon it into glasses and serve warm.

Just before serving, sprinkle each dessert with toasted coconut and spoon over some yoghurt, if you like.

Frozen Watermelon with Minted Sugar

This is so easy to put together, and it's great to make with kids. The hardest part is slicing the watermelon and skewering the pieces to place in the freezer. It's the ideal dessert to serve after a spicy and heady meal, or it makes a great summer treat on those muggy afternoons when you need something fresh and cooling.

SERVES 8

PER SERVING:
CALORIES 124KCAL
FAT NONE
SUGAR 28G

1 medium watermelon, peeled and sliced into small wedges
120g unrefined golden caster sugar

large handful of mint leaves

wooden ice lolly sticks (or reusable ice lolly bases)

• •

Push a wooden lolly stick (or a reusable ice lolly base) into the base of each wedge of watermelon. Place on a tray and freeze overnight.

Using a pestle and mortar, bash the sugar and mint leaves together until you turn the sugar a brilliant green colour.

Remove the frozen watermelon wedges from the freezer and lay on a large serving platter. Sprinkle over the minted sugar and serve.

Sweet and Sour Griddled Pineapple

This dessert is a favourite of mine and I cook it regularly when friends and family are over. If the kids are going to get stuck in too, I leave out the chilli flakes. All my friends have loved it and it's a proven recipe to impress. I've been making this recipe for years now, and the contrast of caramel sweetness from the griddled pineapple, with sour lime and tamarind, plus the extra sweetness of the agave, creates an explosion of wonderful flavours in the mouth!

SERVES 4

PER SERVING:
CALORIES 185KCAL
FAT 1G
SUGAR 36G

zest of 1 orange
juice of 2 oranges
zest and juice of 1 lime
2 tbsp tamarind paste
1 tbsp ground mixed spice

pinch of dried chilli flakes,
    plus extra for sprinkling
1 fresh medium pineapple,
    peeled, cored and cut
    into spears
2 tbsp agave nectar

In a large sandwich bag, combine the orange zest and juice, lime zest and juice, tamarind paste, mixed spice and chilli flakes. Add the pineapple spears and massage until all the pieces are covered in the citrus mixture.

Heat a large griddle pan over a medium to high heat until hot. Remove the pineapple from the marinade (reserve the marinade) and add the pieces to the hot griddle pan in a single layer. Cook for around 2 minutes on each side until nicely charred, turning once.

Add the agave nectar and leave it to bubble for a minute or so, then remove from the heat. Sprinkle with extra chilli flakes and then drizzle over the reserved marinade. Serve warm.

Tropical Fruit Mess

There is no harm in taking short cuts when you are making meals. Here my failsafe short cut is to buy pre-made meringue nests so that I can use them in desserts like this. Keep them in an airtight container once you've opened the packet so they retain their crunch.

SERVES 4

PER SERVING:
CALORIES 194KCAL
FAT 1G
SUGAR 35G

300g 0%-fat Greek-style yoghurt
zest and juice of 1 lime
100ml mango purée (you can use tinned mango purée such as Alphonso, or blitz fresh ripe mango flesh in a food processor)

1 large ripe mango, peeled, stoned and cut into cubes
2 kiwi fruit, peeled and sliced into rounds
¼ fresh pineapple, peeled, cored and cut into cubes
2 meringue nests, crushed

• • • ·· • · • · • ·· • ·· • · • ·· • · • · • · • ·· • · • ·· • ·· • ·· • ·· • ·· •

Combine the yoghurt and lime zest and juice in a bowl. Gently fold through the mango purée to create a marbled effect.

Layer the fruits in individual glasses, spoon the marbled yoghurt over and then finish with some crushed meringue on top.

Cover and chill in the fridge for up to 2 hours, before serving.

Lychee and Coconut Milk Cups

Last year I did a pop up for which I experimented using agar agar, as we often use this as a setting agent for Mauritian jellies and desserts. Initially when I developed this recipe I wanted to set it as a panna cotta, but after playing around I decided to omit the cream and use reduced-fat coconut milk instead, which gave it a crisp texture that melts in the mouth and bathes the tongue with a wonderful floral lychee flavour. When I did the pop up it was a hot summer's night. I served this at the end of a tasting menu that was packed full of spice and chilli, and a lot of people said it was a great way to end the meal.

SERVES 6

PER SERVING:
CALORIES 80KCAL
FAT 1G
SUGAR 17G

450ml light coconut milk
2 tbsp unrefined golden caster sugar
1 tbsp agar agar flakes

3 tbsp lychee syrup from the tin of lychees
15 tinned lychees, drained and halved

Place the coconut milk, sugar and agar agar flakes in a medium, heavy-based saucepan. Bring to the boil over a medium heat without stirring, then reduce to a simmer and stir until the agar agar flakes and sugar have completely dissolved. Remove from the heat and stir in the lychee syrup.

Place 4 lychee halves in the bottom of 6 teacups (reserve the last remaining 6 halves for garnish). Pour over the lychee-scented coconut milk, dividing it evenly between the teacups.

Leave to cool to room temperature, then chill in the fridge for 2 hours until set. Top each cup with half a lychee and serve.

Rainbow Cake

This is a recipe that I made for the Crown Prince of Thailand while I was cooking in an overseas challenge for *MasterChef*. The temperature was about 50°C and I was cooking in a kitchen I'd never worked in before, and for a Prince! It was the biggest challenge of my life, but I remember being so proud of it. It's different to what we think of as cake in the West. It is set more like a jelly as it is made of rice flour and tapioca flour, and it is gluten- and dairy-free. I love the texture of this cake along with the beautiful colours – you can play with the colours and increase the layers depending on how much of an impression you want to make. The main thing you need to make it is patience, but the end result will make you beam with pride!

The best way to measure this cake is using the American-style 'cup' measurement (I use a standard 250ml US cup). I find this is a failsafe approach, and it takes away the drama of scales not working!

SERVES 10

PER SERVING:
CALORIES 245KCAL
FAT 4G
SUGAR 13G

1 cup glutinous rice flour (see Note overleaf)
2/3 cup tapioca flour (see Note overleaf)
½ cup unrefined golden caster sugar
½ tsp salt

1 x 400ml tin light coconut milk, plus 1 cup (about 650ml in total)
2 food colourings of your choice
2 tsp coconut essence (see Note overleaf)
2 tsp lychee essence (see Note overleaf)

• •

Grease a large (23cm) loaf tin with vegetable oil and set aside.

In a large jug, mix together the two flours, sugar and salt until well combined. Stir in the coconut milk and mix until thoroughly combined – you can do this by hand but you need to make sure that the batter is smooth and lump-free. Now pour half of this mixture into another jug, so you now have 2 jugs of batter.

Add a food colouring of your choice and the coconut essence to the first jug of batter and mix. Add a different food colouring and the lychee essence to the second jug and mix.

Place the loaf tin in the middle of a metal steamer. Pour about 2.5cm of hot water into the bottom of the steamer, then place over a medium to high heat (you'll need to keep this level of hot water in the bottom of the steamer throughout cooking, so top it up when necessary).

Now you can begin layering your cake by pouring one-third of the first batter evenly into the base of the loaf tin. Cover with the lid and steam for 5 minutes.

As you open the lid, you can check the first layer is cooked by pressing the top of the batter, it should be firm to the

Recipe continues overleaf

Rainbow cake *continued*

touch. Using some kitchen paper, wipe the top of that layer with kitchen paper to get rid of any moisture, as well as the lid of the steamer, then pour one-third of the second batter (which will be the other colour) evenly over the first set layer. Remember to check the water level at the bottom of the steamer and top it up if necessary.

Cover and steam in the same way; the next layer will take 8 minutes to steam. Continue in the same way, alternating between the two batters, wiping away the excess moisture and then steaming each additional layer for 8 minutes, until all the batter is used up and you have finished steaming the final layer.

Remove the cake from the steamer (leave it in the tin) and leave to cool to room temperature, before placing it in the fridge to set, around 4 hours.

Once the cake has set, the best way to remove it from the tin is to carefully run a palette knife around the edges to loosen it, then turn it out onto a platter. You'll notice that the cake is very sticky but don't worry, this is normal. The best way to slice the cake is to use a hot knife; place the knife under hot water then wipe dry with a clean tea towel before cutting.

I love to serve this cake with fresh fruit scattered on and around it and a sprinkling of sesame seeds.

NOTE
You can buy the flours from health food shops or specialist Asian supermarkets, and the essences online.

Five-spice Stone Fruit

I find that when I buy stone fruit at the supermarket one of two things always happens: the fruit is either over-ripe, or it's under-ripe and never seems to ripen no matter what I do! This recipe makes use of those sour and hard stone fruit, and transforms them into a warming pud.

SERVES 4

PER SERVING:
CALORIES 140KCAL
FAT NONE
SUGAR 32G

100g unrefined golden caster sugar (or depending on how ripe and sweet the fruit are)
juice of 1 lemon
1 cinnamon stick
10 fennel seeds
1 star anise
2 cloves
3 Sichuan peppercorns
4 fresh under-ripe apricots, stones in and skin on
4 under-ripe plums (any type), stones in and skin on

• •

Place the sugar in a heavy-based saucepan with 1 litre cold water, bring to the boil and boil briefly until the sugar has dissolved. Add all the remaining ingredients, then reduce to a simmer and cook, uncovered, for 45 minutes.

Remove from the heat. Transfer the stone fruit from the poaching liquid to a plate using a slotted spoon and set the fruit aside to cool. When they are cool enough to handle, peel off and discard the skins, then set the fruit aside in a serving dish.

Meanwhile, return the syrup to a high heat and leave it to boil and reduce until thickened, around 5 minutes.

Pour (or strain) the syrup over the fruit and serve.

Strawberry and Melon Salad with Black Pepper and Ginger Syrup

A really refreshing summer fruit salad, perfect for a BBQ or a big gathering with friends. It's so easy to prepare, and you can simply tumble the fruit onto a big serving platter.

SERVES 8

PER SERVING:
CALORIES 98KCAL
FAT NONE
SUGAR 21G

40g unrefined golden caster sugar
7.5cm piece of fresh root ginger (peel on), washed and thinly sliced
6 black peppercorns
1 honeydew melon, peeled, seeded and sliced
450g strawberries, hulled and quartered
a pinch of freshly ground black pepper
mint leaves, to decorate

• •

To make the syrup, put the sugar, ginger and peppercorns in a heavy-based saucepan along with 200ml cold water and bring to the boil. When the syrup is bubbling and the sugar has dissolved, remove from the heat and leave to cool until still warm.

Arrange the melon slices and strawberries on a big serving platter. Pour over the syrup and then sprinkle with the ground black pepper. Scatter over some mint leaves to decorate and serve.

Raw Chocolate and Cinnamon Torte

I ate this many years ago with a friend who had started a vegan supper club. I didn't quite understand how it was made and was intrigued to try the recipe for myself. It's an interesting and delicious dessert that will have people asking how you managed to make it without using the oven or heating any of the ingredients. You'll need to start this the day before you want to make and serve it, as the almonds and cashew nuts are soaked overnight before use. This is very rich, so you'll find that a little goes a long way and you can keep servings small.

SERVES 12

PER SERVING:
CALORIES 445KCAL
FAT 33G
SUGAR 16G

FOR THE BASE
250g whole blanched almonds, soaked in cold water overnight, then drained
100g (stoned weight) medjool dates, stoned
pinch of salt

FOR THE CHOCOLATE AND CINNAMON TOPPING
300g cashew nuts, soaked in cold water overnight, then drained
100g unrefined golden caster sugar
100g good-quality unsweetened dark/bitter cocoa powder
100ml coconut oil, melted
1 tbsp ground cinnamon
pinch of salt
mixed fresh berries and shavings of good-quality dark chocolate (70% cocoa solids is preferable), to decorate

• •

Grease a 20cm round cake tin with a removable base and line it with parchment paper. Set aside.

To make the base, place the soaked almonds, the medjool dates and salt in a food processor and blitz to form a soft dough. Press the dough over the base of the cake tin to form the base of the torte and leave to chill in the fridge, while you prepare the topping.

To make the topping, place all the ingredients (except the berries and chocolate shavings) in the same food processor along with 150ml cold water and blend until completely smooth and combined. Pour evenly over the base, then freeze for about 4 hours.

To serve, carefully remove the torte from the tin and transfer to a plate, then decorate with fresh berries and shavings of dark chocolate.

Orange Blossom and Rose Crème Brûlée

There is something so seductive and moreish about crème brûlée, with its silky smooth vanilla-infused baked custard and topping of burnt caramel that you can't wait to crack with the tip of your spoon. Typically this is an indulgent treat, but with a few small changes, this version is much lighter than a traditional crème brûlée, and there is no baking. It is also wonderfully fragrant with arabesque scents of rosewater and orange blossom, giving the sensation of indulgence without the guilt or regret.

SERVES 4

PER SERVING:
CALORIES 239KCAL
FAT 14G
SUGAR 8G

225ml semi-skimmed milk
100ml single cream
1 tbsp cornflour
1 tbsp custard powder
2 egg yolks
1 tsp good-quality
    vanilla extract

150g reduced-fat crème fraîche
½ tsp rosewater
½ tsp orange blossom water
4 tsp unrefined golden
    caster sugar

•••

Pour 200ml of the milk and all of the cream into a saucepan and bring just to the boil – as soon as bubbles appear on the surface, remove from the heat.

Put the cornflour and custard powder into a bowl, add the remaining 25ml milk and stir together until smooth and combined. Whisk in the egg yolks and vanilla extract, then slowly whisk in the hot milk and cream mixture. Return this mixture to the pan and simmer over a low heat for 10 minutes to cook the custard, stirring all the time. Once cooked, the mixture will be thick (much thicker than a custard, but this is fine).

Remove from the heat and stir in the crème fraîche, rosewater and orange blossom water. Spoon the mixture into 4 ramekins, dividing it evenly. Leave to cool to room temperature, then chill in the fridge for 4 hours.

Just before serving, sprinkle a teaspoon of sugar evenly over the surface of each crème brûlée, then caramelise with a chef's blowtorch (alternatively, place under a very hot grill for a few minutes until the sugar melts, turns golden and starts to bubble). Serve immediately.

Luscious Baked Tapioca Pudding

This nursery-style pudding is ideal for families and kids, and immediately takes me back to being a child. It is also great because it's low in fat and gluten free, and is packed full of warming spice plus the sweet hum of vanilla.

SERVES 8

PER SERVING:
CALORIES 213KCAL
FAT 4G
SUGAR 18G

FOR THE PUDDING
200g dried tapioca pearls
75g unrefined light
    muscovado sugar
1 litre skimmed milk
1 vanilla pod, split in half
    lengthways and seeds
    scraped out
1 cinnamon stick

FOR THE TOPPING
3 tbsp desiccated coconut
1 tbsp unrefined golden
    caster sugar

Preheat the oven to 180°C/gas 4.

Place all the ingredients for the pudding in a heavy-based saucepan. Bring to a gentle boil over a medium heat, then reduce the heat and simmer for about 20 minutes, or until the mixture starts to thicken, stirring frequently. Remove from the heat and transfer to an ovenproof dish.

To make the topping, combine the desiccated coconut and caster sugar. Sprinkle this evenly over the top of the pudding. Bake in the preheated oven for 25 minutes until golden brown.

Serve with fresh fruit and reduced-fat crème fraîche, if you like.

Frozen Fruit Pops

All you need are two ingredients for this recipe; it's that easy, and couldn't get any simpler. You can make these with your kids, and they are great for children's parties and BBQs. Made in advance and left in the freezer, these will keep for up to a month. You can use a range of fruits and yoghurts of your choice, but this is the base recipe. You'll also need some wooden skewers for threading the fruit.

SERVE ABOUT 2 POPS PER PERSON

PER SERVING (2 POPS):
CALORIES 62KCAL
FAT NONE
SUGAR 10G

a variety of prepared fresh fruit of your choice, sliced decoratively or cut into chunks

1 x 250g tub 0%-fat Greek-style yoghurt

• •

Line a baking tray with parchment paper and set aside.

Thread a fruit slice or chunk onto each wooden skewer. Dip the fruit skewers into the yoghurt to coat the fruit all over, then place them in a single layer on the baking tray.

Place in the freezer for 2 hours, or until the yoghurt is frozen and firm, then serve.

NOTE
If storing the fruit pops in the freezer, once they are frozen, transfer them to an airtight container and eat within 1 month.

Halo Halo FILIPINO ICE DESSERT

When I was younger I used to go to Filipino parties in London. I absolutely loved going to these parties and I remember I would just walk around and look at all the food on display, noodles, grilled meats and fresh and exotic fruits, and then there was this dessert, Halo Halo. I remember my first mouthful slightly confused me, as there were sweetened beans and I think it was purple yam, but at the same time it was drowned in evaporated and condensed milk, and also included fresh fruit, shaved ice, jelly and ice cream! I've lightened this up, but it still delivers a taste that transports me back to being a kid in the middle of a big festival, clasping this cup of magic with a spoon firmly in the other hand.

SERVES 4

PER SERVING:
CALORIES 237KCAL
FAT 4G
SUGAR 35G

75g unrefined golden
    caster sugar
1 tbsp agar agar flakes
1 tsp natural food colouring
    or vegetable colouring of
    your choice
1 tbsp good-quality vanilla
    extract

50g long-grain white rice
1 large ripe mango, peeled,
    stoned and cut into 5cm cubes
8 fresh lychees, peeled, stoned
    and chopped
1 mugful of shaved ice
    (see Note below)
200ml light coconut milk

Measure 430ml cold water into a medium, heavy-based saucepan, stir in the sugar and cook over a medium heat until the sugar has dissolved. Reduce the heat to a simmer, add the agar agar flakes and stir until the flakes have dissolved.

Remove from the heat and stir in the food colouring and vanilla extract, then pour into a shallow dish. Leave to cool to room temperature, then chill in the fridge for about 1 hour until set. Once the jelly is set, remove it from the dish and chop into rough cubes.

Meanwhile, put the rice into a small frying pan, place over a high heat and let the rice toast for a few minutes until lightly browned all over, shaking the pan a little. Remove from the heat and pound the toasted rice to a coarse, even texture using a pestle and mortar. Set aside.

To assemble the desserts, you will need 4 margarita (or similar) glasses. For each dessert, layer some mango and lychees at the bottom of the glass, then top with some shaved ice, some cubes of jelly and 50ml of the coconut milk. Top each dessert with a little more shaved ice, then sprinkle over the toasted rice and serve immediately.

NOTE
To make shaved ice, you can either place ice cubes in a food processor and blitz to get fine ice, or you can buy it ready-prepared from some supermarkets.

CONDIMENTS

There are certain dishes that just wouldn't be the same without a condiment or sauce. There are some condiments in my house that I literally can't live without, and some meals just don't feel right without them. Every country has their go-to condiments and for me it has to be something pickly, spicy and hot.

Condiments really do help to carry flavour, and those on the following pages are no exception. You can use these alongside other recipes in this book and they are mostly very simple to make, but they do require some store cupboard thought or maybe a trip to the shop to stock up on some key ingredients. Once you have made the condiments, you will be able to store them in the fridge and go to them whenever you want to liven up your meals.

The best part of preparing your own condiments is that you can make them according to taste adding more or using less of certain ingredients, but most importantly, you can monitor what goes into them. A lot of shop-bought condiments contain hidden sugars, salts, fats and additives, so making your own from scratch will give you healthier and more vibrant additions to your meals.

Harissa NORTH AFRICAN CHILLI PASTE

Harissa is really versatile and can be used to spice up a variety of dishes like meat and fish, couscous and even vegetables. Once you have made it, you can cover it with a layer of olive oil and it will keep in an airtight container in the fridge for up to 2 weeks. You can obviously buy your own from the supermarket as there are plenty of good-quality pastes, but making your own at home saves you money as well as allowing you to monitor the amount of salt and oil that goes into it.

MAKES 250ML

PER TABLESPOON:
CALORIES 69KCAL
FAT 7G
SUGAR NONE

20 dried red chillies
7 garlic cloves, peeled
2 tbsp ground coriander
2 tbsp ground cumin
1 tsp fennel seeds
150ml extra virgin olive oil, plus extra for drizzling on top
salt

• •

Put the dried red chillies into a bowl, cover with hot water and leave to soak for 30 minutes. Drain the chillies, reserving some of the soaking liquid.

Put the drained chillies into a food processor along with the garlic, ground spices, fennel seeds, the measured oil and salt to taste. Blitz to combine, adding a little of the reserved chilli soaking water if the paste is too thick.

Transfer to an airtight container, drizzle a small amount of extra olive oil on top to keep it fresh, then cover. This will keep for up to 2 weeks in the fridge.

Raita with Pomegranate and Mint

Raita is a refreshing yoghurt sauce, and this version has a nice fruity twist. It is perfect as a low-fat accompaniment to grilled meats and salads. It also works really well as a dip at parties to serve alongside dishes such as Hara Bhara Kebab (see page 129).

MAKES ABOUT 500G

PER TABLESPOON:
CALORIES 17KCAL
FAT NONE
SUGAR 2G

1 tbsp cumin seeds, toasted
   (see page 17)
1 pomegranate
450g 0%-fat Greek-style
   yoghurt
2 tbsp freshly chopped
   mint leaves

1 tsp chaat masala
   (see Note below)
squeeze of fresh lemon juice
salt and freshly ground
   black pepper

Using a pestle and mortar, grind the toasted cumin seeds to a coarse powder. Set aside.

Cut the pomegranate in half, and then using a wooden spoon, hit the skin of each pomegranate half – this will encourage the seeds to come out. Once the seeds are all removed, try to pick out all white pith as it is really bitter and not very pleasant to eat.

Whisk the yoghurt in a bowl, then stir in the mint, chaat masala, pomegranate seeds and ground cumin seeds. Season with salt and pepper, squeeze over the lemon juice and then serve immediately, or cover and chill in the fridge before serving on the same day.

NOTE
Chaat masala is an Indian spice mix that is quite sour in taste. You can use dried mango powder instead, or you can omit it from this recipe if you prefer. Both chaat masala and dried mango powder are available from specialist Asian supermarkets or international food stores.

Garlic and Mint Dressing

This is perfect served with grilled meats or party nibbles, or as a dressing for a simple green salad.

MAKES 150ML

PER TABLESPOON:
CALORIES 10KCAL
FAT 1G
SUGAR 0.3G

leaves from a large bunch of mint
1 garlic clove, peeled
2 tbsp red wine vinegar
1 tbsp olive oil
1 tsp unrefined light muscovado sugar
100ml boiling water
salt

• •

Place all the ingredients in a food processor and blitz until you get a coarse mixture.

Check the seasoning and adjust to taste with salt and a little more vinegar, if necessary, to get the right balance of flavours. Serve.

Fresh Mango and Lime Dipping Sauce

This is seriously so easy to make. It's a chop-and-blitz condiment that is packed full of fresh fruity and spicy flavours, and it's highly nutritious and low in fat too. I love serving this with grilled meats and as a dipping sauce for finger food.

MAKES ABOUT 300ML

PER TABLESPOON:
CALORIES 8KCAL
FAT NONE
SUGAR 2G

2 ripe medium mangoes, peeled and stoned
1 red pepper, seeded
1 banana shallot, peeled and halved
1 medium red chilli
4 tsp fresh lime juice
salt, to taste

• •

Place all the ingredients in a food processor and blitz until completely smooth.

Serve immediately, or store in an airtight container in the fridge for up to 3 days.

Sweet Chilli and Pineapple Sauce

This sweet chilli and pineapple sauce is a great, healthy alternative to a sweet and sour dressing you would typically get in a Chinese restaurant. It's packed full of natural sweetness from the pineapple, it's really simple to make and I've even used tinned pineapple to make life easier.

MAKES ABOUT 500ML

PER TABLESPOON:
CALORIES 10KCAL
FAT NONE
SUGAR 2G

½ x 435g tin pineapple, drained and chopped
5cm piece of fresh root ginger, peeled and grated
2–3 garlic cloves, finely chopped
2 tsp tomato ketchup
2 tsp cornflour
1 tsp hot chilli powder

Put all the ingredients into a saucepan with 125ml cold water. Bring to the boil over a medium to high heat, stirring constantly so the mixture doesn't catch on the bottom of the pan.

Remove from the heat, pour into a warm, sterilised jam or Kilner jar or a condiment bottle, leave to cool, then cover. Store in the fridge for up to a week.

Coconut Chutney

This is a mellow chutney, yet pungent from the black mustard seeds, and it goes really well with the Grilled Herrings with Kaffir and Chilli brunch recipe (see page 34).

MAKES 500ML

PER TABLESPOON:
CALORIES 23KCAL
FAT 2G
SUGAR 1G

450g low-fat natural yoghurt
6 tbsp desiccated coconut
2 medium red chillies
1 tbsp black mustard seeds
salt, to taste

Place all the ingredients in a food processor and blitz until combined.

Serve immediately, or cover and chill in the fridge before serving on the same day.

Soy and Ginger Glaze

This glaze is perfect brushed over fish or meat before it is grilled or baked in the oven. It's so simple and easy to prepare, and keeps in the fridge for up to a week. A perfect go-to glaze whenever you need to spice things up during the week.

MAKES 200ML

PER TABLESPOON:
CALORIES 14KCAL
FAT NONE
SUGAR 3G

250ml dark soy sauce
2 tbsp clear honey

7.5cm piece of fresh root ginger, peeled and finely grated

· ·

Put the soy sauce, honey and ginger into a pan and cook over a low to medium heat until the mixture has reduced and become thick enough to coat the back of a spoon, around 5–7 minutes.

Once the glaze has thickened, remove it from the heat and leave to cool. Use as required or store in an airtight container in the fridge for up to a week.

North African-inspired Simple Salad Dressing

When I was in Morocco, I loved the playful amounts of cumin and fruit you find in dishes, and I also love pairing fruit with salads. This dressing works particularly well as an alternative dressing for the Beetroot and Orange with Pimento recipe (see page 71).

MAKES ENOUGH TO SERVE 4

PER TABLESPOON:
CALORIES 55KCAL
FAT 6G
SUGAR 1G

2 tbsp olive oil
2 tbsp freshly squeezed orange juice
½ tsp ground cumin

½ tsp paprika
pinch of cayenne, or to taste
salt, to taste

· ·

Place all the ingredients in a small bowl and mix together until completely combined. Taste and adjust the seasoning. Serve immediately.

Nam Pla Prik

I remember seeing this condiment everywhere in Thailand – a watery-looking condiment with the hottest chillies swimming seductively on the surface. The first time I tried it I experienced a major hot chilli sensation on my lips and tongue, beads of sweat appeared on my brow and I got the biggest punch of flavour in my mouth! Even though it was hot, I couldn't get enough of it because it was so moreish, so when I got back to the UK I figured out a way of making it. I still can't get enough of this stuff!

Needless to say it isn't for the faint-hearted, but on your adventurous days I'd absolutely recommend it. I would advise using a mini chopper to prepare this so that you don't end up with all that chilli on your hands, but it is really all according to taste so use as much or as little chilli as you like. This is ideal served as a side condiment with any rice dish or with the Hainanese Chicken recipe (see page 83).

MAKES ABOUT 200ML

PER TABLESPOON:
CALORIES 4KCAL
FAT NONE
SUGAR 0.3G

10–15 red or green bird's eye or Thai 'scud' chillies
1 banana shallot, roughly chopped
2 garlic cloves, roughly chopped
4–5 tbsp fish sauce
juice of 2 limes
100ml water

Place the chillies, shallot and garlic in a mini chopper and pulse together until you get a coarse-looking paste that still has some 'bits' in. Add the fish sauce, water and lime juice and pulse one more time to combine.

Serve immediately, or store in an airtight container in the fridge for up to 5 days.

Brussels Sprout Kimchi

This recipe was born over Christmas. I was experimenting with vegetables and the classic combination was sprouts and chestnuts, but during this same month I remember being obsessed with Sriracha (see opposite) and so my idea for Brussels sprout kimchi was born. This is perfect served with cold meats (and is also great for a lunchbox or for a light bite). Once you have made this kimchi, you can keep it in the sealed jars in your fridge for up to 2 months.

MAKES ENOUGH
TO FILL A 1-LITRE
KILNER JAR (OR
4 X 250ML JARS)

PER TABLESPOON:
CALORIES 6KCAL
FAT 0.3G
SUGAR 0.3G

5 tbsp salt
500g small Brussels sprouts, trimmed and halved
½ small onion, chopped
2 spring onions, sliced
6 garlic cloves, peeled
7.5cm piece of fresh root ginger, peeled and roughly chopped

3 tbsp Sriracha (see opposite)
2 tbsp fish sauce
2 tbsp coriander seeds, crushed
2 tbsp fennel seeds, crushed
1 tsp Kashmiri chilli powder or Korean red pepper powder

• •

In a large saucepan of boiling water, blanch the Brussels sprouts for 1 minute, then remove the pan from the heat and set aside to cool.

Meanwhile, in a large bowl, combine 1 litre cold water with the salt to make a brine. Add the blanched, drained Brussels sprouts to the brine and top with a plate to keep the sprouts fully submerged. Leave at room temperature for 4 hours, then drain (reserving the brine solution in a jug), rinse and set aside in a clean bowl.

Place all the remaining ingredients (excluding the brine and the sprouts) in a food processor and blitz to make a coarse paste.

Add the paste to the drained brined sprouts and combine, then transfer to sterilised jars (a 1-litre Kilner jar is ideal for this, or use 4 x 250ml jars, if you prefer). Pour the reserved brine solution over until it covers the sprouts by 2cm and they are completely submerged. Cover and seal.

Leave the jars of kimchi out in the kitchen for 2–3 days (not in direct sunlight) to allow the kimchi to ferment, then transfer to the fridge. Store unopened jars in the fridge for up to 2 months. Once opened, keep in the fridge and use within 1 week.

Sriracha

Last year I fell in love with this sauce and it quickly became my staple condiment that appears in most of my meals. It reminded me of when my brother was a child and he used to eat ketchup with everything, including curry and rice! Anyway, this is a staple sauce that I love to use to spice up a lot of my dishes, from stir-fries to marinades. It's even good served on its own as a dipping sauce as it's wonderfully fiery, sharp and sweet and satisfies so many taste sensations. I would strongly advise wearing rubber gloves during the preparation of this sauce!

MAKES 1 LITRE

PER TABLESPOON:
CALORIES 45KCAL
FAT 4G
SUGAR 2G

150ml olive oil
2 banana shallots, finely chopped
5 garlic cloves, finely chopped
12 red chillies (Thai 'scud' or bird's eye chillies are perfect for this), finely chopped (seeds left in)

75g tomato purée
75ml fish sauce
75ml rice wine vinegar
3 tbsp unrefined light muscovado sugar

Heat the oil in a pan, add the shallots and garlic and cook slowly over a medium to low heat until softened. Add the chillies and tomato purée and cook for a further few minutes, stirring occasionally to ensure the mixture doesn't stick to the pan.

Remove from the heat, add the fish sauce, vinegar and sugar and stir. The residual heat from the pan will dissolve the sugar. Leave to cool.

Once the mixture has cooled, transfer it to a mini chopper or food processor and blitz to a smooth sauce.

Serve immediately, or store in an airtight container in the fridge for up to 2 weeks.

Index

Acknowledgements

Thanks to:

Jonathan Conway and Jonny McWilliams for continued
support and guidance throughout this book and my career,
as well as The Shine & MasterChef team.

Katie Inglis for inspiring me to really push myself to get
to a goal weight I'm happy and content with.

The team at Ebury and Smith and Gilmour for producing
a wonderful book and supporting me in getting the book
just perfect.

Martin Poole for his amazing photographic skills and Aya
Nishimura for always making my food look sensational.

My biggest inspiration – my Mum and my siblings Kev,
Jim, Pam and Iva, and my beautiful and crazy little nephews.

To all my family and friends in the UK and Mauritius who
support me in all I do.

To my noor for guiding me every step of the way.